Chanukah

EIGHT NIGHTS OF LIGHT
EIGHT GIFTS FOR THE SOUL

Chanukah

EIGHT NIGHTS OF LIGHT
EIGHT GIFTS FOR THE SOUL

Shimon Apisdorf

LEVIATHAN PRESS
BOOKS THAT MAKE A DIFFERENCE

Chanukah
Eight Nights of Light, Eight Gifts for the Soul
by Shimon Apisdorf

Copyright © 1997 Shimon Apisdorf

Leviathan Press
2505 Summerson Road
Baltimore, Maryland 21209
(410) 653-0300

Notice of Rights

ISBN 1-881927-15-6

Printed in the United States of America
First edition
Cover illustration by Julius Ciss (416) 784-1416
Cover and jacket design by Bill Hackney at Staiman Design
Page layout by Fisherman Sam
Hebrew typography by Mendelsohn Press
Research services by Gail Schiller
Technical consultants: E.R./D.L./Y.B.Z.
Editorial services by Sharon Goldinger/PeopleSpeak

Distributed to the trade by NBN (800) 462-6420

All books from Leviathan Press are available at bulk order discounts for educational, promotional and fund raising purposes. For information call (800) 538-4284.

Other books by Shimon Apisdorf

Rosh Hashanah Yom Kippur Survival Kit (Benjamin Franklin Award)
Passover Survival Kit
The Survival Kit Family Haggadah
The One Hour Purim Primer: Everything a family needs to understand, celebrate and enjoy Purim.
The Death Of Cupid: Reclaiming the wisdom of love, dating, romance and marriage. By Nachum Braverman and Shimon Apisdorf

More praise . . .

The Death of Cupid is an insightful guide to discovering the beautifully deep potential of marriage.

John Gray, Ph.D., <u>Men Are From Mars, Women Are From Venus</u>

The relevance of the Passover Seder comes to life with this excellent, well written guide.

Detroit Jewish News

This exciting spiritual approach to taking the old and making it new has inspired me to reexplore my Jewish values.

Deena Kranitz, JCC Young Adult Program Coordinator

The Rosh Hashanah Yom Kippur Survival Kit is fun, meaningful and brilliantly written. If I had the resources, I would buy a copy for every Jew in America.

Rabbi Ephraim Z. Buchwald, National Jewish Outreach Program

Response was great. I wish I could get this into the hands of every Jewish college student across the country.

Sarah Rosenthal, Director of Campus Youth Services, Bergen County Jewish Federation

For the first time in my life I realized that Judaism could actually be relevant.

Todd J. Appelbaum, Columbus Jewish Federation Board of Trustees

DEDICATED WITH LOVE, TO MY WIFE MIRIAM.
A RADIANT SOURCE OF LIFE AND LIGHT.

ACKNOWLEDGEMENTS

Donna Cohen, Helen and Joe Berman, George Rohr, Oscar Rosenberg,William Schottenstein, Arthur Rosenthal, Rabbi Michel and Rebbetzin Feige Twerski, Jake Koval, The Efrons, Michael Monson, Rabbi Menachem Goldberger, Yechezkal Mordechai Nemani. Reuven, Jenny and Benyamin. Dov Friedberg, Mike Schatel, Shifra Strauss, Barry and Rita, Jaclyn and Jason, Yehudis Silverstein, Russell and Julie,Uncle Harry, Aunt Leslie and ZoZo, Sharon Goldinger, Isaac, Rinat and Family, Bill Hackney, Julius Ciss, The Yards.

APPRECIATION

Ann Apisdorf, sister, friend and chavrusa. Asher Resnick, a friend whose mesiras nefesh is woven into the lines of this book. Josh Greenberg. Sam Glaser, music for the soul. Rabbi Yaacov Weinberg shlita. Aish HaTorah, my teachers and friends. Rabbi Noah Weinberg, Rosh Hayeshiva and source of inspiration.

SPECIAL THANKS

My parents, David and Bernice Apisdorf. "Ordinary" people who do extraordinary things. Where would I and many others be without you?

Mr. and Mrs. Robert and Charlotte Rothenburg. Pillars of love and loyalty.

Esther Rivka, Ditzah Leah and Yitzchak Ben Zion. Each a gift. Each precious. Each a shining little light.

Miriam. Because of you, this book was written. Because of you, we share the light of our inheritence. Because of you, we merit a home filled with light—and simcha!

Hakadosh Baruch Hu, source of all blessing.

CONTENTS

The goal of this book is to peel away the outer layers of Chanukah, the wrapping paper if you will, and reveal a profoundly rich, spiritual core to the holiday. Chanukah is about the awesome subtleness of life. It's about the power in a diminutive flame to banish a world of darkness. It's about discovering the soul in the flame, the soul in everyday life and the power of the soul in Jewish history.

THE GRINCH WHO STOLE CHANUKAH

A few years ago the religion editor of a metropolitan newspaper called me to discuss a piece she was working on about the upcoming holiday season and to gather some material about Chanukah. She wanted to know if I could provide her with a different "take" on the holiday than she was used to hearing. "And what is it you're used to hearing?" I asked. "Well, you know," she said, "the people I talk to every year tell me either that Chanukah celebrates the struggle for national self-determination or else that it's a time of giving, like Christmas and Kwanzaa, only in a Jewish sort of way."

To be honest, I don't remember what my response was or what she eventually wrote in her seasonal article. My "take" however, on the holiday of Chanukah can be found between the covers of this book.

Let's begin by making one thing clear. If no one gives or receives even one present on Chanukah, they have not omitted or missed out on anything central to the holiday. The holiday of Chanukah has little if anything to do with the giving and receiving of gifts. Chanukah is not the Jewish season of giving. If any Jewish holiday could be construed to be the holiday of giving, it would be Purim—which does not happen to be celebrated around December 25—and not Chanukah, which usually arrives around the same time as Santa.

Having said that, please don't think that you've just met the Grinch who stole Chanukah. I'm not a sullen old kill-joy and the goal of this book is not to drain the fun out of Chanukah but rather to peel away the outer layer, the wrapping paper if you will, and reveal a profoundly rich spiritual core to the holiday. This book will help you find insights within the Chanukah celebration that can illuminate important issues that we all struggle with in life. It will also help you uncover ancient spiritual pathways that grow out of the practices that do make up the essence of the Chanukah celebration. Through your discovery of deeper layers of meaning contained within every facet of Chanukah you will gain a new "take" on this wonderful holiday; and perhaps on your ultimate potential as a Jew and a human being. I hope that after having read this book you will come to appreciate Chanukah not as a season of giving but as a season of growing. It is a time for acquiring fresh insights into Jewish life and a bold new inspiration for living. And what greater gift, after all, could there be?

BASEBALL AND THE JEWISH HOLIDAYS

To a baseball fan there is nothing quite so magical as opening day. Opening day, the first day of the baseball season, represents the vitality of fresh potential. A new line-up of players—of potential—prepares to take the field. It's a crisp spring afternoon; the harsh winds of winter are but a fading memory, the President himself winds up to throw the first pitch—and anything is possible. Opportunity fills the air. It's time for each player to try it all again, to give it his very best shot and to set his sights on nothing less than the World Series.

Every Jewish holiday is opening day for a new season of spirituality. Every holiday is a fresh encounter with a familiar experience and new opportunity for insight, for personal growth and for reaching new levels of spirituality. At the same time, no two holidays are alike. Each comes with its own distinct opportunities and potential. Each calls our minds to consider and contemplate particular ideas; each asks us to assess and further develop aspects of our character; each asks us to pause and reflect upon life through a uniquely Jewish lens; and each calls out to our souls and asks us to lift our eyes, discover the presence of God in our lives and strive to become more of who we want to be and who we can be.

Every holiday is a season brimming with fresh opportunities. The Passover Seder is opening day for the season of freedom. The first time someone walks into a *sukkah* it's opening day for the season of joy. The lighting of the first Chanukah candle is opening day for the season of soulful living.

THE SOUL OF CHANUKAH

Chanukah is about two ever present forces: darkness and light. It's about a struggle between two world shaping ideologies: Hellenism and Judaism. It's about the imperceptible human spark that enables people to reach far beyond their perceived limitations. It's about the power in a diminutive flame to banish an enormous darkness. It's about a tiny people that is able to overcome the most daunting of foes.

Chanukah is about the awesome subtleness of life. It's about how little things can make a profound difference, and it's about discovering the soul in the flame, the soul in everyday life and the power of the Jewish soul in history.

Presents are wonderful—to give and to receive. And *latkes*—well, to many of us they are the taste of heaven itself. The goal of this book is to introduce you to dimensions of Chanukah that will broaden the parameters of your holiday experience. In so doing it is my hope that you will discover a new, more spiritually inspiring context that will give new meaning to Chanukah, and even to its presents, and add a fresh taste to every batch of latkes.

THE STORY OF CHANUKAH: FOR THE HISTORICALLY CHALLENGED

There were only two types of students in the high school I attended: those who found history class to be intolerably boring ("Who caaares what happened in 1491? What does it have to do with me?") and those who actually enjoyed memorizing long lists of names, dates and bygone events. If you were among the handful of history buffs in your graduating class, then you can skip this chapter. However, if the mention of a clash between the Trojans and the Spartans evokes images of the Rose Bowl, if the word Acropolis reminds you of your favorite Greek restaurant and if you can't remember if it was Antiochus, Achashverosh or Aristophanes who married Queen Esther, then you will find the following historical overview and summary helpful.

HELLENISM AND WESTERN CIVILIZATION: WHO CARES?

Hellenism, the culture that blossomed in Athens, is the primary source of western civilization. In many ways we in the United States are the cultural by-products of a far more influential society than our own—that of ancient Greece. Before the Greeks, everyone who lived in Europe was unlettered, uncultured and somewhat barbaric.* It was the Greeks, and after them the Romans (Roman culture was an extension of Greek culture), who brought philosophy, the study of history, schools, athletic competition, sophisticated literature, poetry, a well-developed theater, architecture, urban planning and the concept of democracy to Europe and eventually, by extension, to America. Historians insist that there is almost nothing in our society (with the exception of Dennis Rodman) that doesn't have its roots in ancient Greece. Consider the United States Capitol building in Washington, D.C. The structural design is a descendent of Greek architecture, the form of government it houses was born in Greece and the logic, philosophy and rhetoric that animate many of its discussions and debates originated in Greece.

> *We ourselves, whether we like it or not, are the heirs of the Greeks and the Romans. In a thousand different ways, they are permanently and indestructibly woven into the fabric of our own existence.*
>
> Michael Grant, *The Founders of the Western World*[1]

---

*The Greek view of the world had little room for other than two types of people: Hellenes, people who had assimilated the manners and mores of Greek culture, and Barbarians, those who were in need of Greek enlightenment.

ZEUS, AND A BIT ABOUT GREEK SOCIETY

In the ancient world, Greece was not a country as we think of one today, but rather a collection of loosely knit and often warring city-states. The two most dominant and best remembered of these city-states were Sparta and Athens. These two regional powers waged an ongoing struggle for control of the Greek peninsula. In the end, Athens was the great victor not only because of the sword and the phalanx, but because its culture, Hellenism, eventually overwhelmed much of the world.

The Greece that has so influenced our world is the Greece of Hellenistic culture, but there was more to Greece—there was the ever-present religion of the Greek gods. The Greeks' world was populated by two races: the godly race and the human race, though the lines could be easily blurred.

It is hard for us to imagine a world populated by the great gods Zeus, Poseidon, Apollo and Aphrodite (not to mention hundreds of others), but make no mistake, the Greeks took their gods as seriously as we take the stock market, the six o'clock news and the personal computer. The gods had their fingers in every aspect of Greek life, literally. These gods were not content with life atop Mount Olympus and, when the urge moved them, would often come down to earth where they would sleep with mortal women, drink with mortal men and murder anyone who offended them.

As Greek society progressed it began to subtly question the position of reverence accorded to the gods. Eventually the Greeks concluded—while continuing to pay reverent homage to the gods—that people were capable of being the equal of, if not superior to, the gods. With time, though the gods and the customs, forms of worship and festivals that surrounded them remained central to daily Greek life, it soon became apparent that the true masters of the world were humans and not gods.

It was the human race, not the god race, that developed philosophy and the arts. It was the human race that began to explore the world of natural science and build beautiful buildings, and it was the human mind and its capacity for creative thinking that was seen as the source of great light that could illuminate the lives of people everywhere. In fact, as art imitates life, this attitude became central to Greek art. "The singular physical character of Greek art was . . . its preoccupation with the human and with the gods' proper place in the world of men (rather than vice versa)."[2]

The fourth and fifth centuries B.C.E. were the golden age of Greek Hellenism. The Greek culture that flourished at this time was rooted in drama and the theatre; in athletic competition, the gymnasium and the glorification of the human body; in political thought and new forms of government, and most of all in Greek philosophy and the veneration of human logic. At the center of this great flurry of cultural development was Athens. It was the enlightened culture of Athens that would eventually conquer the world, and it was this same culture that would ultimately clash with Judaism at the time of Chanukah.

ALEXANDER THE GREAT

In 338 B.C.E. Philip of Macedon invaded Greece from the north and absorbed Athens and the Greek states into the Macedonian empire. Two years later Philip died and his son Alexander assumed the throne. Alexander was enamored with Greek culture, revered Homer and was greatly influenced by the thinking of Aristotle with whom he had a personal relationship. According to the Greek historian Plutarch, Alexander had "a violent thirst and passion for learning . . . he was a lover of reading and knowledge." Alexander's grand design was not only to rule vast areas of land but also to make Hellenism the preeminent cultural force in the world.

Alexander the Great was a conquerer unlike any other who had ever lived. His meteoric rise and seemingly invincible military prowess made him a legend even while he was still alive. The empire of Alexander the Great eventually stretched from Macedonia and Greece across the conquered Persian empire and all the way to the frontier of India. Included in this vast empire were Egypt and Israel, which was then regarded as part of Syria. When Alexander's troops reached Jerusalem, the Jewish people offered no resistance. It was the forces of Alexander that first brought Hellenism to Jerusalem and the Jewish people.

Thirteen years after coming to power, at the age of thirty-three, Alexander the Great was dead.

WHY CAN'T YOU BOYS JUST GET ALONG

No other two races have set such a mark upon the world. Each of them from angles so different have left us with the inheritance of its genius and wisdom. No two cities have counted more with Mankind than Athens and Jerusalem. Personally, I have always been on the side of both.[3]

Sir Winston Churchill

Though the Jewish people put up no resistance when Alexander's troops arrived, they were quick to resist the enlightening cultural forces that the Greeks brought with them. The question is why? The Jewish people were a people who revered education, literacy and deep thinking. In this regard the Greeks should have been their soul mates, another enlightened people in an otherwise darkened world. This was not, however, how the Jews saw things. When it came to Hellenism, the cultural glory of Greece and a force that would truly shape the minds of men for thousands of years to come, most Jews had one response: resistance. And that was a problem because it was a type of resistance that the Greeks weren't used to. To resist military domination was one thing, but to resist and reject the beauty of Greek theatre, the glory of olympic competition and the profundity of philosophy was something altogether different. In a sense, the Jews became the Greeks harshest enemies because rather than rejecting the strong arm of the Greeks, they rejected its heart and soul— its culture.

Again, however, we are left with the question why? Why was it that the Jews felt compelled to reject Hellenism? What was it about this culture that the Jews couldn't tolerate?

THE DARK SIDE OF GREECE

For all its beauty, Greek society also had numerous prominent aspects that would be absolutely abhorrent to most people today and were certainly abhorrent to the Jews of two thousand years ago.

In Greek society it was as common for parents to kill a newborn infant as it is for us to send out birth notices. Babies in Greece were routinely murdered by leaving them outside in a clay jar to die from exposure and starvation. The reasons parents would kill their children were many. Too many mouths to feed was one reason; too many heirs for a father to divide his estate among was another. Sickliness was certainly grounds for exposure, and in a society that revered the beautiful form of the human body (and where public male nudity was not uncommon), deformity was also grounds for exposure. The great philosopher Plato suggested that families should be limited in size by law to one boy and one girl. To a Jew, no matter what else Greek culture stood for, if it was capable of legitimizing wholesale infanticide, then it was a bankrupt culture.

Right behind infanticide on the list of what we today consider deviant behavior was pederasty. We call it child molesting. "In most Greek communities the women were kept at home and men spent their days with other men or boys. Artists paid special attention to the nude masculine form; and pederasty abounded. It was far more favored than homosexual relations between men and youths of the same age, and indeed a whole philosophy was built up around the pederastic situation, founded on the concept that the lover was the beloved's educator and military trainer."[4] Again, for us it is virtually impossible to conceive of a "philosophy" that justified and even glorified the man-boy relationship, but in Greece there was a general understanding that the highest and purest form of love was something we consider to be the most henious of crimes.

The Jewish people are, and even two thousand years ago were, a people that placed the utmost value on human life and that considered the relationship between a husband and a wife and parents and children to be holy. Such a people just couldn't tolerate a society in which infanticide and pedophilia as well as the advocation of adultery and institutionalized prostitution existed. But there was more.

A PHILOSOPHICAL CLASH

Two of the predominant ideas in Greek philosophy, ideas that were fundamental to the Greek world view, were the concepts of forms and function. So what's a form and what's a function you ask? And why did these ideas bother us Jews so much? Well, it goes like this:

Forms are the objective, absolute and immutable qualities that are the true definition of any concept. Let's take a concrete example—for instance, a peach. A peach can exist in various dimensions. First, it is a tangible physical object, a piece of fruit. Then, at the same time, there is the concept of what a peach is, and this conceptual peach exists independently of the object itself. You see, the Greek philosophers wanted to know why it is that when I say peach and you hear peach, what we are both thinking of is a peach and not a watermelon. Their answer was that we share a common concept of what a peach is. That shared concept was known as its form. But they didn't stop there. Those brilliant Greek philosophers took this idea further and drew the following conclusion: The only truly perfect peach is the form of the peach, all other peaches, no matter how delicious they were, were only approximations of the perfect concept of a peach. Therefore, they concluded, the way to evaluate how "good" a peach was is to first understand the abstract form called peach, and then to evaluate all peaches in relation to that form. Now you are probably thinking, "So what? So the Greeks were deeply into philosophizing about what makes a good peach. What's the big deal about that?"

The problem was that they took this notion of forms and extended it from peaches to people and used it to determine what it was that made a person good. Which brings us to the concept of function.

The idea of function asserts that everything has a function, that which it is uniquely suited for and does best. For instance, the function of a nose is to smell. True, you might be able to balance a spoon on your nose, but that is not what it uniquely does best. Other things are more adept at balancing spoons, while nothing detects smells better than a nose. So the *function* of a nose is to smell and the *form* of a nose is the abstract concept of the appendage of perfect olfactory capability. Which brings us to human beings.

> *Why not live the Playboy life? Because, says Plato, the highest good for anything, human or nonhuman, consists in fulfilling its own nature, in living up to its own form or essence.*[5]

> T.Z. Levine , *From Socrates to Sartre*

The function of a human being, above all else, said the Greeks, is the unique ability to use language and to reason. The capacity to reason, to think logically and to communicate such thoughts through language is the distinguishing characteristic of human beings. Thus, the Greeks concluded, just like a good nose is the nose that is well developed in terms of its ability to smell, so too a good person is the person with the well-developed faculty of logical reasoning. And since happiness is an outgrowth of fulfilling one's function, the happy man is the man of reason and logic.

These ideas of form and function bothered the Jews for a number of reasons. First, this philosophy asserts that nature is the final determinant as to what a person ought to be doing in life and what it is that makes a person virtuous and good. Second, this philosophy concludes that it is within man's ability to understand the purpose of all things and what it is that gives anything its value and meaning. To the Jew, the basic issues of what gives a human life value and meaning, what determines who is or is not a good person and what it is that represents the goal of human existence are derived from a transcendent God who is the source of nature and of all existence.

> *The Hellene [Greek] loved reason as much as form, and boldly sought to explain all nature in nature's terms.[6]*
>
> Will Durant, *The Life of Greece*

The Greeks saw the human mind as the ultimate tool to fathom the will of nature. The Jews see the human mind as a gift to use to fathom the will of the Creator. One world view is nature and man centered and the other is God centered. And that's a big difference.

PTOLEMY, SELEUCUS AND ASSIMILATION

The Jewish resistance to Hellenism set the stage for two conflicts. One was internal, between Jew and Jew, and the second eventually grew into an armed Jewish revolt against the Greeks.

With the death of Alexander and the absence of a natural successor, Alexander's empire was divided among his leading generals. Antigonus controlled Macedonia and Greece; Seleucus controlled Babylonia, Persia and Syria (excluding the area of Israel); and Ptolemy controlled Egypt and Israel.

Ptolemy, like Alexander, was a lover of Hellenism. The empire he established dominated Israel for almost a century. The Ptolemaic rulers were at times tyrannical in their advocacy of Hellenism and at times tolerant of Judaism. It was during this period that large numbers of Jews began to assimilate Greek culture into their lives. This group was known as the Hellenists.

Despite the fact that in many ways Hellenism and Judaism were at seemingly unreconcilable odds with one another, still, powerful political and social forces were at work that made Hellenism attractive to many Jews. First, "The only way to gain entry into the new system of power lay in the adoption of Greek culture."[7] A Jew with ambition during the time of the Greeks had no choice but to join the local gymnasium, buy a season pass to the theater and maybe take up writing poetry as a hobby. (What some people won't do to fit in.) Additionally, it is clear that there was a very seductive dimension to this bold new culture.

> Greek culture was so lively and fun. It had theatres and athletics, some fancy books, and a refined style of dining, the symposium. [At the symposium men were often attended to and entertained by beautiful women.] By comparison it must have been rather dull to be a Jew in the evenings before the Greeks came.[8]
>
> The Oxford History of Greece and the Hellenistic World

And finally, in truth, all that was Greek was not bad. Far from it. Probably no other people in history other than the Jews has revered learning and wisdom as the Greeks did. In laying the foundations for democracy, the Greeks asserted that people were not just cogs in the wheel of state but that each individual had the right to determine his own future. There was nothing anti-Jewish in this idea. And was there anything really so objectionable with the Greek emphasis on beauty, athletics and the arts? What's so terrible about, "my son the sculptor," "my son the architect" or for that matter, "my son the javelin thrower." For the Hellenist Jews, Greek culture represented the way of the future and was the door through which they could gain entry to the halls of power in Greek society.

Though the great majority of Jews remained loyal to the Torah and Judaism, the rise of Hellenism inevitably led to internal Jewish struggles. Not only did the confrontation with Greek culture open the doors of assimilation, but it also planted the seeds of a deep schism within the Jewish people. In the end, the Jewish war against Greece at the time of Chanukah would prove to be not only a war of Jew against Greek but also a war between Jew and Jew fought over the heart, soul and future of the Jewish people.

The year 199 B.C.E. was a turning point. In that year, the Seleucid dynasty that ruled from Antioch in Syria wrested control of Israel from the Ptolemies. It was under the Seleucids that harsh decrees were issued against the practice of Judaism. All Jews were required to follow the lead of their Hellenist brethren and embrace Greek culture. It was then that the study of Torah and the observance of Judaism brought with it the risk of death. The dual forces of Hellenist assimilation and Syrian-Greek oppression posed a great threat to the continuity of traditional Jewish life.

Mattisyahu and the Jewish Revolt

Jerusalem, the spiritual center of Judaism, with its Temple, great Torah academies and large Jewish population, was the natural target for the fiercest enforcement of the anti-Jewish decrees. To drive their point home the Greeks built a gymnasium, one of the central symbols of Greek culture, right next to the Temple. Eventually they would insist that a statue of Zeus be placed in the Temple itself. For those reasons Mattisyahu, the scholarly and righteous scion of the Hasmonean family, moved his family out of Jerusalem to Modiin. But the reign of terror followed them there too.

One day the Greek forces arrived in Modiin and insisted that the Jews offer a sacrifice to a pagan god. Mattisyahu, as a respected elder, was singled out to be an example for the other townspeople, but Mattisyahu was defiant. Mattisyahu refused to be intimidated, but while he stood strong another Jew stepped forward to offer the sacrifice. An enraged Mattisyahu grabbed a sword, killed the renegade Jew and then turned on the Greek soldiers. Soon the small band of Greek soldiers lay dead on the ground in Modiin. The Jewish revolt had begun.

The elderly Mattisyahu died within a year and never saw the success of the revolt he began. After the passing of Mattisyahu, his son Judah took over as leader of the family and of the revolt. A brilliant tactician and leader, Judah organized a fighting force known as the Maccabees. It was under the inspired leadership of Judah Maccabee that the Jews were able to successfully confront the Greeks and eventually recapture the Temple. When the victorious Jewish forces entered the Temple they found one small flask with enough oil to kindle the great Menorah for just one day. And then a miracle happened: One day's supply of oil continued to burn for eight days.

The rest of the story, as they say, is history.

HISTORICAL OVERVIEW

The following charts are designed to give you a sense of the flow of events that took place during the period of Chanukah and to place them in the broader context of Jewish history. While the story of Chanukah is about the Jewish encounter with the great civilization that was Greece, when looking at the chart of Jewish history one sees how the Jewish people also came face to face with the Babylonians, Persians, Romans, French and Russians to name just a few. A fascinating and perhaps even miraculous history.

OVERVIEW
JEWISH HISTORY

Abraham and Sarah	2080/1671 BCE
Egyptian slavery begins	2332/1428 BCE
Exodus and	
Torah at Mt. Sinai	2448/1312 BCE
Jewish People enter Israel	2488/1272 BCE
First Temple built	2935/825 BCE
First Temple destroyed;	
Babylonian exile begins	3338/422 BCE
Purim events	3405/355 BCE
Second Temple built	3408/352 BCE
Miracle of Chanukah	**3597/165 BCE**
Second Temple destroyed;	
Roman exile begins	3830/70 CE
Babylonian Talmud compiled	4260/500 CE
First Crusade	4856/1096 CE
Expulsion of French Jewry	5155/1475 CE
Rise of Chassidism	5532/1772 CE
First Zionist Congress	5657/1897 CE
Holocaust	5698/1939 CE
Rebirth of Israel	5708/1948 CE
Reunification of Jerusalem	5727/1967 CE
Mass exodus of Russian Jews	
to Israel begins	5750/1990 CE

OVERVIEW
CHANUKAH PERIOD

Athens defeats Persia	
at Marathon	490 BCE
Plato; Greek philosophy	404 BCE
Sparta defeats Athens	400 BCE
Second Temple built	3408/352 BCE
Philip of Macedon conquers	
Athens and controls Greece	338 BCE
Alexander the Great rules	
Macedonia/Greece	336 BCE
Alexander dies; Ptolemies	
control Egypt and Israel	323 BCE
Seleucid Syrian/Greeks	
conquer Israel	199 BCE
Greek decrees against Judaism;	
desecration of Temple	3594/168 BCE
Mattisyahu begins revolt	
in Modiin	3595/167 BCE
Mattisyahu dies; Judah Maccabee	
leads Hasmonean family and	
war against Greeks	3596/166 BCE
Temple recaptured; miracle	
of the oil occurs	**3597/165 BCE**
Jewish war against the	
Greeks continues	165-140 BCE
Hasmonean dynasty	140-36 BCE
Rome conquers Jerusalem	3698/63 BCE

EIGHT QUESTIONS PEOPLE ASK ABOUT CHANUKAH

(I)

Question: Why do we celebrate Chanukah for eight days?

Answer: When the Temple stood in Jerusalem, one of its central elements was the golden Menorah. There was a special obligation to light the Menorah every day. In lighting the Menorah, only specially prepared oil could be used as the fuel. This oil took seven days to prepare. It was the finest oil and produced the clearest of flames; nothing else would do.

The Jews recaptured the Temple from the Greeks and sought to reinstate the daily activities. The first thing they did was to light the Menorah, though they had only one flask of oil, enough to last for just one day. After the Menorah was lit a miracle happened. Instead of burning for just one day, the flames of the Menorah stayed lit for eight days, long enough for new oil to be produced. Today we light our menorahs for eight days to recall this miracle and to be inspired by its message.

Insight: When the Temple stood in Jerusalem, it played a central role in the spiritual life of the Jewish nation. Whenever a Jew wanted to express special feelings of closeness to God, he or she could present an "offering" in the Temple (the Hebrew word for offering is *korban,* which means "to draw close"). Three times a year all Jews would gather together at the Temple to experience the inspiration of being a part of the Jewish people. And every single day, the golden seven-branched Menorah was kindled in the Temple.

The Menorah and its flames represented the light of Torah wisdom: the soul of the Jewish nation. Every day the Menorah was rekindled as a reminder that each and every Jew needs to take daily steps toward lighting his or her own inner flame by exploring the Torah's wisdom for life.

The Greeks, against whom the Jewish forces were waging war, saw Judaism as their enemy. Unlike Haman and the Persians in their time (the Purim story) or Hitler and the Germans in their time, the Greeks did not want to exterminate the Jews; rather, it was Judaism as a way of life that the Greeks were opposed to.

When the Jews liberated the Temple from the Greeks, they immediately sought to reinstate the daily lighting of the Menorah. They searched the Temple grounds for the flasks of specially prepared olive oil that were used to kindle the Menorah, but the Greeks had done a thorough job when they ransacked the Temple, and all the Jews could find was one small flask of oil—enough to fuel the Menorah for just one day. The Jews were elated to find even this one container, yet their joy was tempered for they knew that after that first day the Menorah would again be lifeless. The process of producing fresh oil for the Menorah would take a week tocomplete. In the meantime, though the Temple had been liberated, the Menorah would have to remain lifeless.

The Menorah was rekindled. All who saw the flames burning again knew that the flame of Jewish life could never be extinguished. And then a miracle happened. The flame would not go out. The flask had contained just enough oil for one day, yet after that first day the flame continued to burn and burn and burn. For eight full days, long enough for new oil to be produced, the Menorah miraculously stayed lit. In their hearts and souls, the Jewish people knew that they had received a special message. They struggled and had done everything in their power to rekindle the Menorah, but all their efforts could produce was one day's worth of light. But they were not alone in their struggles. God had responded to their heroic efforts and enabled the flame that they lit to burn on and on for eight days.

Even today the Jewish people seem to face an impossible challenge: A tiny and often powerless people is asked to keep the unique flame of Judaism burning in a world that is often at odds with Jewish ideas and ideals. The miracle of Chanukah says to us: don't look at the odds against you, look only at the task in front of you. The challenge of the Jew and of the Jewish people is to keep the flame of Torah and Judaism burning brightly in an often dark and hostile world. We do the best we can to rise to the challenge, and when we reach the limits of our ability we must know that God will step in to assure our success. As long as Jews never give up, the Jewish flame will never be extinguished.

(II)

Question: Why do people often place their menorahs near a window?

Answer: There is a *mitzvah* (a commandment or spiritual directive) to light the menorah every night of Chanukah. Part of the procedure for lighting the menorah involves lighting it in such a way that "publicizes the miracle." In order to fulfill this aspect of the mitzvah, people place their menorahs in front of a window so that the flames are visible to the public.

It's true that by placing one's menorah in the window the miracle of Chanukah is clearly publicized; however, there is another possible location for the menorah that is considered even better for publicizing the miracle. Jewish law states that ideally, the menorah should be placed outside the front door of one's home on the left side of the door as one enters. In fact, today in Israel many homes are constructed with little cubby-holes in the wall next to the front door where menorahs can be placed. These cubbies have glass doors that keep out the wind or rain and enable all who pass by to see the flickering lights of the menorah. It is a beautiful experience to be out on the streets of Israel watching families gathered at their front doors to light the Chanukah menorah.

Insight: I. "TO PUBLICIZE THE MIRACLE"

One can have different "takes" on the Jewish people and Jewish history. One might see us as the Wandering Jews, as the People of the Book, as the fountainhead of all monotheistic religions, or as the Eternal Nation. The concept of publicizing the miracle of Chanukah calls our attention to another perspective on the Jewish people: the partnership perspective. The awareness that says; we're not in this alone.

The Jewish people have always understood their identity as being defined by a relationship and partnership with God. As such, one of the defining elements of Jewish consciousness is the presence of a miraculous wrinkle in our history.

Let's go back to the origins of the Jewish people. The couple that founded the Jewish people, Abraham and Sarah, had already been senior citizens for decades when their son Isaac was born. There was simply no room in nature for Isaac to be born, but he was. The nation that began with a couple of ninety year olds who could not have children, but did, was destined to be a people that should not be, but is. If there is a "survival of the fittest" element in history, then large and powerful empires like the Greek's, Roman's, Ottoman's or Russian's should still be alive and kicking; but they are not. The Jews have outlived them all. A tiny group, scattered, despised and persecuted, the Jewish people have not only survived and made numerous contributions to civilization along the way, but thousands of years after the conquest of ancient Israel, a remnant returns to do what no other conquered people has ever done before: reclaim and rebuild its homeland. The Jewish people should have vanished ages ago, but thanks to a historical partnership— and miracles—we're still around to light our menorahs, spin our dreidels, enjoy our latkes and publicize the miracle.

Insight: II. CHANUKAH AND THE FAMILY

"Family values" has become the social issue du jour. Many people will tell you that almost all the major ills present in our society can be traced to a breakdown in the fabric of our families and a general loss of family values. In a not so subtle way, Chanukah is about family values as well as the value of the family.

As was mentioned, the ideal place for a menorah is at the left side of the door as one enters a house. In addition to publicizing the miracle, another idea that factors into this placement. The menorah is positioned in this fashion so that the entrance to one's home will be "surrounded by mitzvot." The menorah will be on the left side of the door and the mezuzzah on the right side. On Chanukah, the symbols and ideas of the mezuzzah, the menorah and the Jewish home are all mingled together.

Every mezuzzah, no matter how simple or elaborate the exterior may be, contains the exact same piece of parchment.

Inscribed on this parchment is the statement of *Shema Yisrael:* "Hear o' Israel, the Lord Our God, God is One." This sentence, along with the two other paragraphs written on the parchment, contains the essence of Judaism. A Jewish home, more than anything else, is meant to be a place for fostering Jewish values and ideals. The mezuzzah on our doorpost reminds us that a home is a place for learning, for growth and for spirituality, not just a shelter from the rain.

In many ways the Jewish home and the Jewish family are central to Chanukah. The revolt against the Greeks was spearheaded by a family, the Hasmoneans. Another family, Chanah and her seven sons (all of whom gave their lives rather than denying their devotion to God), stand as the ultimate symbol of dedication to Judaism. According to Jewish law, one should always try to light the menorah when the entire family is gathered together. The Talmudic terminology for the obligation to light the menorah on Chanukah is *ner ish u'bayso,* "one candle for each man and his household."

During Chanukah, one's front door, the entranceway to Jewish family life, is to be surrounded by mitzvot. The mezuzzah calls our mind to the values and ideals that are taught and discussed and lived in a Jewish home, while the menorah reminds us of the willingness of the Jewish people, and particularly of Jewish families, to fight for the survival of the Jewish home and Jewish life.

The story of the Jewish people is the story of the Jewish family. We are a nation of families and a family that is a nation. For the Jewish people, Jewish survival and Jewish revival begin and end in the Jewish home.

Chanukah is an appropriate time for families to think about what they can do to enhance the Jewish dimension of their lives. Here are some ideas:

1) Put aside twenty minutes a week to read a Jewish book with your children.
2) Light Shabbat candles on Friday night with your daughter.
3) As a family, visit a nursing home. Find out who has no one to visit them and bring them a card at the next holiday. Children can make their own cards.
4) *Tzedakah* (charity) and the stock market:
   Stocks are an investment and *tzedakah* is too. As a family, choose one or two charitable causes that you would like to help and then put aside a jar in your kitchen into which everyone can deposit some money on a regular basis. Once every few of months, gather the money and send it to the organization. Each time you send in the funds, include a note asking if there is any new information about the activities of the cause you are supporting. When that information arrives, read it together and watch your investments grow.
5) If you are single, your house is still a Jewish home and an important part of the Jewish family of homes. There are many things you can do to enhance the Jewish character of your home. You can put a mezuzzah on your doorpost, hang a Jewish calender in your kitchen or start building your own Jewish library. Try designating one bookshelf in your home for your Jewish library, and once a month buy a book to add to your collection.

(III)

Question: Do you have to use colored candles when you light a menorah?

Answer: Without a doubt, there is something special about those colored candles we all grew up with. However, not only are colored candles not a requirement, you don't even have to use candles at all if you don't want to.

"You mean I can use leftover sparklers from the Fourth of July?"

Actually, that would be going too far, but what you can use is olive oil. In fact, because it was used in the original Menorah in Jerusalem and because it produces such a beautiful flame, olive oil is considered the fuel of choice for the Chanukah menorah. Another advantage of oil menorahs is that you can add fuel to them and keep those tiny flames burning throughout the night. This helps maintain the Chanukah atmosphere in your house long after the lighting ceremony has ended.

Insight:

> *By perseverance the snail reached the ark.*
>
> Charles Haddon Spurgeon

> *Never give in.*
>
> Sir Winston Churchill

The olive and its oil are symbolic of the Jewish people. Think about it. Do you know how you get the finest oil from an olive? You've got to press it really hard.

Life creates a lot of pressure, and it is often precisely at those times when we have been pushed to the breaking point that our finest moments shine through. To persevere and overcome enormous pressure is one of the defining challenges of life. It is also a defining theme in Jewish history.

The Jewish people have carried a love for Jerusalem through centuries of oppression by enemies who swore we would never see her walls again. The Jewish people have been called upon to believe that the value of all human beings lies in their being "created in the image of God," despite being victimized by the most evil and grotesque of men. Jewish parents have even educated their children to be proud, committed Jews when being a Jew was a liability at best and a mortal danger at worst.

When the Dalai Lama was exiled from Tibet, he sought out the council of Jewish leaders. The Jews are mankind's paradigm for perseverance.

This is the message of the olive, its oil and the clear flames of the menorah. The harder you try to crush our bodies and souls, the brighter our flame will ultimately shine.

TO MEDITATE ON THE FLAMES

One is not supposed to use the lights of the menorah for any type of personal benefit. Not to read, not to help light a room, nothing. There is a song that is sung after lighting the menorah known as "These Lights" (*Ha'neiros Ha'lalu*), and in that song you will find the words "These lights are holy and we are not permitted to use them, rather, all we can do is look at them."

"All we can do is look at them." The flames of the Chanukah menorah can serve as the focus for uplifting, even transcendent, meditation and contemplation. Go ahead, give it a try.

> ### A MEDITATION
>
> On Chanukah, late at night, sit down in front of your menorah and just gaze at the flames. Tiny, silent flames. Glowing, sometimes dancing; vulnerable, yet always reaching upward. You too possess an inner flame. As you look at the flames of the menorah, as you begin to notice every nuance and detail, allow yourself to feel your own inner flame. Tiny, silent flame. Flame that is often lost in the swamp of so many things to do. Flame that wants to dance, to reach upward, to touch something higher and richer and deeper. That flame is your flame. And it can never be extinguished.

(IV)

Question: Why do we spin a dreidel on Chanukah?
Answer: Quite frankly, that's not an easy question to answer because in Judaism, even something as "simple" as kids playing a Jewish version of spin-the-top is really not as simple as it appears to be. Let me explain.

As we discussed in the introduction, Jewish holidays are not just commemorations of historical events. Every holiday is a unique island of spirituality that offers a special opportunity for insight, growth, inspiration and a deepening of one's connection to God.

In the world of interior decorating we understand why a corporate office is furnished differently than a dining room and why a family room will look very different from a bedroom. Each is appointed in such a way that best serves the intended function of the room. The same is true when it comes to Jewish holidays. Everything about a particular holiday is designed to create a customized environment that is best suited for experiencing, absorbing and becoming absorbed in the opportunity of the holiday. The spiritual furnishings that create a holiday's atmosphere are made of things such as *mitzvot* (command-ments), special prayers, meals, selected portions of the Torah that are read and studied, songs and customs. Which brings us back to our question of the dreidel: In what way does the custom of the dreidel contribute to the spiritual atmosphere and oppor-tunity of Chanukah?

At times in our history, Jews were imprisoned for the "crime" of studying the Torah. Chanukah was one of those times. While in jail, these Jews would gather together to play dreidel. Under the guise of idling away their time on a simple game, they would engage in discussions of Torah topics and thus continue to defy the enemies of Judaism. The game of dreidel reminds us of our eternal defiance of anyone who tries to stand between a Jew and the Torah.

Insight:

> Since all of life is futility, then the decision to exist must be the most irrational of all.
>
> Emile M. Cioran

> Life is like a top; you spin around a lot and then you fall over.
>
> Anonymous

To some, life is a game. To others it's a joke, and to still others it's an arbitrary abyss. Not to the Jewish people. The Jewish people have been "spinning" through history for three thousand years. To some, Jewish history, like life itself, is little more than an arbitrary string of events—events whose frequent tragedies seem to proclaim life's futility—but the message of Chanukah and of the dreidel is just the opposite.

Every dreidel has four sides with one Hebrew letter written on each side. Each of these letters is the first letter of a word.

The four letters are *nun* (the first letter of the word *nes*, which means "miracle"), *gimel* (the first letter of the word *gadol*, which means "great"), *hey* (the first letter of the word *hayah*, which means "was") and *shin* (the first letter of the word *sham*, which means "there"). When taken together these letters proclaim "A great miracle happened there."

In Jewish mystical teachings, there is another dimension of meaning to the dreidel and these four letters. The dreidel presents an image of Jewish history, and the four letters represent four different historical empires (Babylonian, Persian, Greek and Roman) that tried to destroy the Jewish people. Today we are still considered to be victims of the Roman Empire because it was the Romans who destroyed the Second Temple and sent us into the exile that we continue to occupy. The issue is this: Is Jewish history just a cruel game? Are we just spinning haphazardly from one tragedy to another, or is there some rhyme and reason to all that has happened in our history?

During the time of Greek oppression, Jews could have easily despaired, seen life as just a game, and given up hope in the eternity of the Jewish people. Like a top, they could have fallen over. But they didn't. They believed that just like a hand spins the dreidel, so there is an ultimate guiding force in history. While the dreidel is spinning, the letters are a blur and no one knows how it will land. Similarly, there are times when it seems impossible to make sense of Jewish history. It is at those times that Chanukah and the dreidel present their message: If we believe that there is ultimate meaning to the Jewish people, if we know that despite the dizzying blur of events in our history there is some purpose to it all, and if we are prepared to fight to remain Jews regardless of what history throws at us, then who knows—we might just see a miracle and be reassured that there is a hidden hand guiding the destiny of the Jewish people.

Less than fifty years ago, for the first time since the Maccabees defeated the Greeks, the Jewish people were on the verge of reclaiming sovereignty in their homeland. Around the world many people were skeptical if the birth of this new state would happen at all; even more were convinced that if it was born, it would soon go down in defeat to the vastly larger and far better equipped Arab armies.

"For political reasons—to convince the world they could not be ignored—the Jews of Palestine had built up an image of strength. So persuasive was their propaganda, even the Arabs had been fooled . . . but reality, as Ben Gurion and a handful of Haganah leaders knew, was pathetically different.

The Haganah had weapons for less than a quarter of its men. Its total arsenal consisted of 'some 8,300 rifles, 3,600 Sten guns, 700 light machine guns, 200 medium machine guns, 600 two-inch and 100 three-inch mortars, all of different types. There was sufficient ammunition for only three days fighting.' Haganah [the fledgling Jewish army] had no heavy armaments of any kind—no heavy machine guns, no artillery, no anti tank or anti aircraft guns, no real armored cars. Nothing whatever to use in the air or on the sea.

Then, on December 5, 1947, the United States made things even tougher for the Jews. Shortly after the U.N. approved the partition of Palestine into two countries, one Jewish and one Arab, the United States government announced a total embargo on arms sales to the Middle East. While the embargo would be fair and apply to everyone in the region, by that time, the Arabs had already purchased tens of millions worth of U.S. arms surplus. In addition, the British continued to sell arms to the Arabs only.[9]

In Israel, in order to be a realist, you have to believe in miracles.

David Ben Gurion, First Prime Minister of Israel

(V)

Question: Why was there a Menorah in the Temple in Jerusalem?

Answer: The Temple in Jerusalem was central to the spiritual life of the Jewish people. Three times a year, on the holidays of Passover, Shavuot and Sukkot, all Jews went to Jerusalem to celebrate the holidays. Imagine the feeling of being together with every Jewish family in the world to celebrate the Passover seder in Jerusalem. When the Temple stood in Jerusalem, the Jewish nation gathered there, together as one, to deepen both their personal and national sense of connectedness to God. It was a place of concentrated spiritual power and electrifying inspiration.

The Temple contained various items that were essential to the activities that took place there. One of these items was the Menorah, which was made of one solid piece of gold. It was ornate in design and stunning to behold. Each of its seven branches was topped by a receptacle that held the oil that fueled its flames. In the Temple there is a special mitzvah for all seven branches of the Menorah to be kindled on a daily basis. This daily lighting ceremony was carried out by a *kohen* and was one of the primary daily activities in Jerusalem. It was also a source of great inspiration to all who contemplated its many layers of meaning.

Insight: WARNING!!! WARNING!!! This is going to be a lengthy insight with some information you may have never heard before, but hang in there, I think you'll find it quite interesting.

PART I. LONG AGO IN A LAND FAR, FAR AWAY

Before the advent of the light bulb, buildings were illuminated by the natural light of the sun. For this reason windows (which were just openings in a wall) were designed so that they were narrower on the outer side of the wall and wider on the inside. This design served as a type of funnel that captured the rays of the sun and then dispersed the light inside the building. Curiously, in the Temple in Jerusalem the windows were designed in the opposite fashion. The Temple windows were narrow on the inside of the walls and wide on the outside. The purpose of this unusual design was to make a statement about the Menorah.

The light of the Menorah represented the light of Torah wisdom. The seemingly backward design of the windows signified that the light of Jewish wisdom was intended to radiate out to the entire world. More than the Temple needed the light of the sun, the world needed the enlightening wisdom of the Torah.

At this point you might be saying to yourself, "Okay, that sounds nice, but what do you mean the Menorah was a source of light for the entire world?"

To answer that, we're going to have to take a look at the Menorah in the broader context of the Temple. (I told you this was going to be a bit long, but if you can keep reading a little longer I think you will learn some neat new stuff about the Torah.)

PART II. INDIANA JONES AND THE TWO TORAHS

As was mentioned, the Menorah represented the enlightening wisdom of the Torah. However, there was another very prominent item in the Temple that represented the Torah even more clearly than the Menorah. This was the Ark (as in *Raiders of the Lost Ark*). The Ark contained two things: the tablets that the ten commandments were written on and the very first Torah scroll ever written. Obviously with these as its contents, the Ark was the primary item in the Temple to represent the Torah. So if the Ark represented the Torah, then why was there a need for the Menorah to also represent the Torah?

If you are thinking that there must have been two Torahs, then you're headed in the right direction. What you are about to discover is a very important, though little known, fact about the Torah. The Torah actually has two parts to it. One part is world famous, has been a bestseller in almost every language and has been read and studied by people of every faith and background. The other part is far less well known, almost defies translation and has been studied by almost no one other than Jews for thousands of years. Part one (the world-famous part) consists of the text of the Torah, is commonly called the Five Books of Moses and is known to mankind as the Bible. It is this text of the Five Books of Moses that is written on every Torah scroll, whether it's that first scroll that was kept in the original Ark or a Torah scroll that can be found in the ark of any synagogue today. In classical Judaism the text of the Five Books of Moses is known as the *Torah Sh'bichtav*, the "Written Torah." Part two of the Torah (the not-so-famous part) is known as the Torah *Sh'baal Peh*, the "Oral Torah." Classical Jewish thought maintains that when the Jewish people received the Torah they not only got two tablets but they also got one Torah in two distinct parts: one part written and one part oral. The written part was, as its name indicates, actually written down so that anyone could read it. The Oral Torah, as its name suggests, was not written down. Its contents were studied, memorized and carefully taught without the benefit of a source text. It was taught, discussed and transmitted directly from teacher to student.

PART III. WHAT'S AN ORAL TORAH?

The oral part of the Torah is the detailed explanation of the text in the Written Torah. Taken on its own, the Written Torah is pretty tough to understand and can even be downright misleading if you don't have the accompanying explanation contained within the Oral Torah. Without the Oral Torah, the Written Torah is alarmingly incomplete. You just can't point to a Torah scroll in synagogue and say, "That's the entire Torah," because it isn't. There is a whole other part of that Torah, the Oral Torah, that completes the unit.

Here are two examples of how this symbiotic relationship between the Written and Oral Torahs works.

I) In the Written Torah there is a section that deals with the issue of compensation when one person injures another person. The Written Torah says that the way to redress the injury is "An eye for an eye and a tooth for a tooth." It would seem reasonable to conclude that this means if you break my arm then either I or the courts can break your arm. This would be justice. However, the Oral Torah explains that this is not the case at all. In fact, based on the Oral Torah's elucidation of the written text, Jewish law deals only with monetary compensation for an injury. *An eye for an eye* was never meant to imply "you broke my arm; now I can break yours," and in Jewish jurisprudence this verse was never applied literally. In Jewish law if you injure me you might have to make payments toward my medical expenses or my loss of income, but you will never have to be injured in return. Someone familiar with only the written part of the Torah would have no way of knowing what applied Jewish law actually is in such cases.

II) A wonderful holiday takes place about a week after Yom Kippur called Sukkot. During Sukkot, families build a temporary dwelling where they eat their meals during the holiday. The Written Torah says, "In sukkot you shall live for seven days." The problem here is that it doesn't tell us what these sukkot are. Are they tents, tepees, igloos or something altogether different from these other ethnic dwellings? If we had nothing other than the Written Torah, then on the holiday of Sukkot, Jews would have built log cabins, lean-tos and probably even customized condos. But they didn't. As it turns out, the Oral Torah spells out quite precisely what a sukkah is. Thanks to the Oral Torah, wherever Jews have lived, their sukkot have always been the same.

So there we have it. One Torah, two inseparable parts. Which brings us back to the Menorah, the Ark and those funny Temple windows. The Ark that contained the tablets and the very first Torah scroll represented the Written Torah, while the Menorah represented the Oral Torah. The tablets and the scroll were kept in a closed Ark because without the benefit of the Oral Torah, the Five Books of Moses are actually the Five *Closed* Books of Moses. The Written Torah is just indecipherable without the Oral Torah.

If it's dark and you want to read, you turn on a light. Beautiful lights shone from the Menorah because it is the Oral Torah that liberates the meaning and the wisdom contained in the Written Torah. The Oral Torah enables the light of Torah to shine forth and be a source of light for the Jewish people and for all mankind.

The windows of the Temple in Jerusalem were backward to signify that more than the Temple needed the light of the sun, an often darkened world needed the light of Torah.

(VI)

Question: Where does the name of this holiday, Chanukah, come from?

Answer: The Hebrew word *chanukah* has various meanings that are each closely related. The word chanukah means "education," "dedication" and "beginning."

When the Maccabees liberated the Temple from the Greeks they found that the holiest place in Judaism had been terribly abused and desecrated. (When the Germans turned synagogues into horse stables and Torah scrolls into lampshades, and when Arabs used Jewish tombstones to pave their roads, they weren't the first to strike at Judaism by striking at her objects of sanctity.) The Temple needed far more than cleaning and repairs; it needed to be rededicated. This *dedication* marked a new *beginning* for the Temple and the Jewish people and is the source of the name of the holiday.

Insight:

> *Educate [chanoch] a child according to his nature; when he grows old he will not abandon it.*
>
> King Solomon, The Book of Proverbs

> *As soon as a child can speak his father must teach him Torah and the Shema.*
>
> Talmud

> *Education is a responsibility incumbent on every father and mother.*
>
> Rabbi Shlomo Volbe

The essence of Jewish parenting is to teach your children what to be dedicated to. The secret of parenting is to understand the nuances of your children's nature and to educate them in accordance with that nature.

While no two children are alike, all children need to be taught that it's wrong to steal. Personalities and temperaments may vary, but the need to be kind, compassionate and moral is universal. One child may be shy, another creative, and still another always in a hurry; yet they all need to learn what it means to be a *mensch*.

Jewish parents are called upon not only to teach their children life-enhancing skills—like eating with a fork and spoon or using a computer—but also to teach those values and ideals that will bring meaning to their children's lives. Just like we don't let them wait to decide when they get older if they want to read or write, we also must not suspend the teaching of values and character until they are old enough to decide for themselves.

It is the responsibility of every parent to teach their children to understand what's important in life and what's not so important, what is of deep and lasting value and what, as fun as it may be, has only limited value; what principles demand dedication and sacrifice; what's morally and Jewishly negotiable and what's not.

I recently received a call from the past. From Cleveland to be exact.

It was an old friend from high school who was serving as the co-chair for our twenty-year reunion. "Everyone is going to be there." He insisted, "Isn't there any way you can make it? It's going to be a great weekend."

I really did want to attend, but unfortunately the main reunion events were scheduled for Friday night and Saturday. I explained to my old friend that since graduating from high school I had begun to observe Shabbat and that even if I made the trip from Baltimore to Cleveland, I'd still have to miss most of the reunion. But that didn't fly. "Perhaps," he wondered aloud, "you could make an exception. I mean if one time you kind of bend the rules a little, would that be so terrible? Look, nobody's perfect."

I told him that I was very touched by his call, that his interest in my presence meant a lot to me, but I just wouldn't be able to make it. "Besides," I told him, "the Indians are in Baltimore that weekend and I have tickets to the game on Sunday."

"Oh, you never told me **that**," he said. "Now I understand. Look, we'll miss you. I gotta go make another call. It's been great talking to you."

At the time of Chanukah the Jewish people fought for the opportunity to rededicate the Temple because they knew what they themselves were dedicated to in the first place.

(VII)

Question: Why do we give presents on Chanukah?

Answer: Everybody I know, including my own kids, is going to feel like strangling me after reading this answer. Before I put my neck on the line, I just want to preface this by stating in my defense that, yes, I got Chanukah presents when I was a kid; no, I don't tell my parents or in-laws not to give gifts to their grandchildren; and yes, my wife and I do give our kids a few gifts on Chanukah.

Having said that, let me now answer the question.

The reason we give presents on Chanukah is because Chanukah always overlaps the Christmas season and we have become culturally overwhelmed by our society's obsession with Christmas presents. We have adopted an "if you can't beat 'em, join 'em" attitude, and thus gifts have become as much a part of Chanukah as they are of Christmas. Don't get me wrong, there is nothing bad about presents per se, it's just that they don't have any particular significance on Chanukah.

So there you have it; and from now on I'm sure there will be people who will refer to me as Shimon "the Grinch who stole Chanukah" Apisdorf.

Insight: There is great historical irony in the fact that Chanukah has been so dramatically impacted by a non-Jewish religion and culture.

The story of Chanukah is the story of a dominant world culture, that of the Greeks, and its attempt to overwhelm Judaism. The Greeks had no interest in killing Jews, and they weren't even interested in killing Judaism. Their interest was in making their culture, Hellenism, the dominant cultural force in the world. They would have been perfectly willing to let the Jews adopt an "if you can't beat 'em, join 'em" attitude in which Jews would keep their Judaism and simultaneously adopt Greek culture. It's not so much that they wanted us to stop being Jews, they wanted us to *also* start being Greeks. It was only when the Jews resisted the introduction of Hellenism into Jewish life that the Greeks felt compelled to outlaw the practice of Judaism. In so doing they went too far and created a situation that eventually led to the Jewish revolt, the war against the Greeks and their imposed culture and ultimately to the miracle of Chanukah.

The Jewish people fought to resist one culture and have celebrated that resistance for over two thousand years. Now we find ourselves adopting the customs of yet another culture to celebrate the victory of Chanukah. I wonder what Judah Maccabee would say about that?

(VIII)

Question: So who was Judah Maccabee anyway?
Answer: Close your eyes and picture Arnold Schwartzenegger: His Uzi has just jammed, he's got one arm in a sling, he's about to take on three hundred bad guys all at once—and he's wearing a yarmulka. That's who Judah Maccabee was!

Two thousand years ago, one family led by one man stood between the mighty Greek army and the conquest of the Jewish people. The family was the Hasmoneans, and the man was Judah Maccabee.

The Greeks were different from other empires. They didn't just want your land, your resources and your riches—they wanted your national essence, your culture. They wanted you to think like them, live like them and even be entertained like them. The problem was most Jews weren't buying, and the

Greeks didn't appreciate that. So the Greeks brought pressure to bear on the Jews. Women who insisted that their sons be circumcised were killed along with their babies. Brides were forced to sleep with Greek officers before they could be with their husbands. Jews were required to eat pork and sacrifice pigs to the Greek gods. The teaching of Torah became a capital crime.

The sages and their students went into hiding in order to study and preserve the Torah. Secret weddings were held. Most Jews did anything and everything to remain Jewish. Many were tortured and murdered for their defiance. A period of darkness and suffering descended upon the Jews of Israel.

And then came the Hasmoneans.

The Hasmonean family was led by Mattisyahu and his five sons: Shimon, Yochanan, Yehudah (Judah), Elazar and Yonasan. Mattisyahu was a devout man who could not bear to see Judaism and the Jewish spirit crushed. It was his family that led the revolt against the vastly superior Greek forces. Mattisyahu understood that the battle was far less for national liberation than it was for spiritual and religious liberation. Though Mattisyahu's valor provided the initial spark for the revolt against the Greeks, he died shortly after the rebellion grew into a full-fledged war. The mantle of leadership passed from Mattisyahu to his son Judah, and with that the course of history was forever changed.

Judah Maccabee was a fearless leader, a brilliant battlefield tactician and a man capable of inspiring thousands to take up arms in the battle for the preservation of Judaism. It was Judah Maccabee who conceived of ways for the Jewish forces to out maneuver the larger, better equipped and seasoned Greek army. When at last the Jews captured Jerusalem, rededicated the Temple and witnessed the miracle of the oil, it was with Judah Maccabee as the leader of the Hasmonean family and at the head of the Jewish army of liberation.

Arnold—step aside!

Insight: If you are traveling somewhere in the world and you want to know if American culture has reached that place, don't look for an American flag, look instead for the "Golden Arches." If McDonalds has arrived, then Steven Spielberg can't be too far behind.

Can you imagine that today there are places in the world where Levi jeans sell for hundreds and even thousands of dollars, that Croatia is starting to produce basketball players talented enough to be NBA All Stars, and that somewhere behind the Great Wall of China there are countless people who can't get enough pirated CDs of rap music?

The Greeks would have been awfully jealous because this is exactly what they were trying to do with their culture. They wanted their philosophy, form of worship, entertainment, arts, literature, theater and athletic games to become the defining elements for peoples national and daily lives everywhere.

At the time of the Greek conquest there were two kinds of Jews living in Israel. First, there were those who decided that Hellenism represented an attractive alternative to Judaism. For them, Hellenist culture was the way of the future, the way to gain acceptance into the larger Greek society and the way to prosperity. Some abandoned Judaism altogether and some relegated it to a secondary role in their lives, but all of them believed that they belonged more to the theater and the gymnasium than to the halls of Torah study and the Temple. These Jews were the Hellenists.

The second group, and the larger of the two, was the traditional Jews—the "ardently orthodox" of their day. This group continued to lead a Jewish life despite the Greek persecution and despite great risk to their very lives. When the Hasmoneans launched their revolt it was this camp that provided the men who would come to be known as the Maccabees. The Jewish rebellion was a great event in Jewish history, but tragically, the war against the Greeks was also a civil war. Not all Jews sided with the Maccabees, who to some represented the past. Many Hellenized Jews aligned themselves with "progress" and with the future. As a result, Jews battled with one another for the right to define the future of Jewish life and the Jewish nation.

In many ways the story of Chanukah is the story of how one man and one family can make all the difference in the world for an entire people. It was the inspiration of Mattisyahu, the leadership of Judah Maccabee and the stubborn tenacity of the dedicated Jews that literally saved the Jewish people and the Jewish way of life.

As a Jew, don't ever think that you can't make a difference.

NIGHTS OF LIGHT, GIFTS FOR THE SOUL

(I)

THAT'S JUST NOT ME

They searched the Temple thoroughly but found only one small jar of oil, enough to burn for one day. A miracle happened; they were able to light from that oil for eight days.

Talmud

Who would have dreamed that within that little jar of oil was a miracle waiting to happen? In a way, we all have something in common with that little jar.

Jewish wisdom has an image of every person: The image is that of a vessel. In some way we are all receptacles. Each of us has the potential to receive or accept spirituality into our lives. However, just as some vessels are more appropriate for certain contents than others, so too certain people seem to be more appropriately shaped—so to speak—for certain types of spirituality than others.

We tend to have very definitive images of ourselves. How many times have you looked at someone who had a particular strength—maybe they are very disciplined or maybe they are very flexible and easy going; maybe they are always up on all the political issues of the day or maybe they never lose their temper—and said to yourself "that's just not me"?

When looking at ourselves as vessels, an important issue that needs to be explored is this: What is it that determines the "shape" of our personal vessels? What makes one of us a cereal box, one of us a wicker basket and another a crystal vase? The answer, of course, is multifaceted.

> In our hands we hold the moist clay of our own lives. Potters of the spirit, we possess a far-reaching ability to shape from everything we are, the vessel we long to be.

The initial mold of our vessel is cast by God. It is then dramatically shaped and worked by our parents, stamped by our friends and society and chiseled here and there by countless life experiences. And then comes our part. Each of us is clearly a central force in molding and shaping ourselves. We each possess a far-reaching ability to make out of everything that we are, the vessel we want to be. As we engage in the process of shaping ourselves, one of the pivotal factors that ultimately determines the nature and contours of our vessel is our self-perception.

Eventually most of us reach a point in life when we look at ourselves and say, "This is who I am." At that moment we unknowingly cross a threshold and in doing so we give a final shape to our vessels—to ourselves. At the moment that we proclaim "this is who I am," we relegate most everything else to the realm of "that's just not me." The spiritual consequence of putting the final touches of self-perception on our vessels is that we have decided which types of spiritual experiences are open to us and which are closed. For some people there is nothing more sublime and inspiring—nothing that touches the soul more— than a stirring piece of Mozart or Yanni; while someone else will decline even the chance to listen to such music because they already know, "that's just not me." For some people it can be a prayer or the sound of the shofar that most fully fills their vessel, while someone else will just look on with a sense of disbelief knowing without a doubt that such things are "just not me."

One of the most powerful principles that underlies Chanukah—and one of the most profound opportunities that it presents us with—is the concept that no matter where we are in life, we still possess the inner ability to recast the form of our vessels. Chanukah is a time when there exists an unusual potential to reshape our vessels and thus enable ourselves to receive all sorts of spiritual gifts that we never imagined we could possess. Chanukah is a time to look again at things that we have declared to be "just not me" and to open ourselves to the possibility that we can still give new lines, textures and dimension to the figure of our vessels; ourselves.

I would like to make the following suggestion as a method for accessing the full potential of Chanukah. Identify two things in life that fall into the "that's just not me" category. Then, sometime during Chanukah, go ahead and do them anyway, with the following attitude: "I always thought that this just isn't who I am but I'm going to give it a try and open myself to whatever the experience has to offer." Of the two things that you try make one of them overtly Jewish, like lighting Shabbat candles Friday evening, attending a class about Judaism or saying a few blessings before and after you eat some of your food one day. The other can be more worldly, like taking a long hike through the woods, visiting a nursing home or writing in a journal.

> *During the eight days of Chanukah the same spiritual lights that were created by the miracle are once again available to every Jewish soul. However, in order to experience and to feel this unique light, we need to detach ourselves from the natural order of things and thereby ready ourselves to receive that which emanates from above the natural order.*
>
> Sefas Emes, early Chassidic master

The story of Chanukah is the story of the defiance of the natural order of things. It is the story of a moment in history when what should have happened didn't, when the ordinary, the expected and the natural were overwhelmed by the extraordinary, the unexpected and the spiritual. The Jewish rebels turned back the mighty Greek army, Judaism and Jewish life survived the onslaught of a culture that changed world history and a small vessel that appeared to contain only a bit of oil became the source for eight days of light.

When we look at ourselves and say "that's me" or "that's not me," we lock ourselves into the world of the ordinary and the expected. Chanukah not only reminds us that there is another dimension to life, but it also asks us to open ourselves up to that dimension by stepping outside of the mold we have created for ourselves. When we dare to defy what we would ordinarily expect of ourselves, when we make an effort to give new shape to our vessels, we then become capable of receiving a light that should only have shined for a day but that in fact continues to shine, even today.

(II)

LOOK AT WHAT YOU ARE LOOKING AT; FEEL WHAT YOU ARE FEELING

FOCUS

How many times have you driven to work and once you arrived realized that you had almost no recollection of the trip? "Highway hypnosis" happens to all of us and not just in the car. The mind, it seems, has a mind of its own. Without even thinking about it our thoughts and musings often put us somewhere other than where we are. We may appear to be working, cooking, watering the lawn, driving on the highway or listening to a child tell us about her day, but in our minds we are elsewhere. We may be somewhere in the past—reliving, rethinking or reviewing some bygone event—or we may be speculating about, planning for or looking forward to the future. The result is that we literally don't see, don't experience, what is right in front of us.

> *For all the eight nights of Chanukah—these lights—they are holy; and we are not permitted to use them: Rather only to look at them.*
>
> *Haneiros Ha'lalu*, Chanukah prayer

The only thing you are allowed to do with the lights of the Chanukah menorah is to see them. On the surface this doesn't seem to be very demanding. However, Judaism considers the ability to see things to be one of the keys to fully experiencing the depth of life and to discovering the spiritual within the mundane. Consider the following:

> *And Moses was shepherding the flock of his father-in-law . . . And he saw, and he was struck because the bush was*

on fire but it was not being consumed. And Moses said to himself, "I will turn aside and I will see this incredible sight—why is this bush not being burned?" And God saw that he had turned aside in order to see, and God called out to him from the midst of the bush and said, "Moses, Moses."

The Book of Exodus

With regard to this very famous story of the burning bush our sages tell us the following: "From here we learn that there is no place that is devoid of God's presence." This in itself is a powerful concept, that spirituality—God's presence—is discernible in all things and all places. That to touch the infinite, the awesome and the transcendent we need not trek to the top of a mountain or the shores of the ocean. Even a thorn bush, the very thing that we pass by every day, that we even try to avoid contact with, is a repository of God's presence. But there is more: "And Moses said to himself, 'I will turn aside and I will see this incredible sight . . . And God saw that he had turned aside in order to see, and God called out to him from the midst of the bush."

Moses made a conscious decision to "turn aside" in order to be able to see the burning bush. The question is, where was Moses' mind before he turned aside to see? Was he thinking about his sheep, was he thinking about his father-in-law, was he thinking about the life he had left behind in Egypt or what the future had in store for him? Wherever Moses' mind was, it required a conscious and directed effort for him to turn his mind from those things and focus on the spectacle in front of him. And clearly, had he not turned aside, he never would have seen the bush. After all, it was the turning aside that caught God's attention ("And God saw that he had turned aside") and led to God calling out to Moses from the midst of the bush.

What we learn then from this story is this: In reality there is nothing mundane in life. That which appears to be quite ordinary, to be lacking depth and meaning, only seems so because we have not yet seen what is truly there. We have not made the conscious decision to turn our attention from the endless stream of thoughts that carry us away from the present in order to perceive the extraordinary that is there in front of us. The story of the burning bush tells us that not only is God's presence in all things, but also that the key to experiencing that presence—to enabling it to call out to us—lies in our ability to focus our minds attention. Which brings us back to another fire: the flame of the Chanukah menorah.

Remember, "For all the eight nights of Chanukah—these lights—they are holy; and we are not permitted to use them: Rather only to look at them." Our relationship to the lights of the menorah is supposed to be one of looking and seeing. We look at the flames of the menorah and we see that they are far more than they appear to be. They are not just candles, not just little flames. They are beacons. They call out to us to turn aside from everything else—from everywhere else—and to see what is really there. Holiness, transcendence, spirituality and Godliness can be present even in a little flame. A flame that can't be used for anything, that is of no more use to us than a thorn bush, that can't help us do anything—but see.

THE BLESSING OF BLESSINGS

In Jewish life we are asked to say lots of *brachot*, blessings. For example, we say very specific blessings before we eat. One for fruit, one for vegetables, one for cookies, another for beverages and so on. There is also a blessing to be said after going to the bathroom, before smelling a rose bush, after one hears a loud clap of thunder, when one sees an unusually beautiful person, when one meets an exceptionally wise person and at a marriage ceremony, to name just a few. Verbally reciting blessings is a prominent feature in Jewish life and is meant to make an indelible impact on our consciousness.

> Blessings are our own voices clothed in the words of the soul. They call our attention to spiritually dramatic moments that often vanish without anyone taking notice.

In Hebrew the word for blessing, *brachah*, is closely related to the word *breichah*, which means a natural spring of water. A free-flowing spring of fresh, life-giving waters is the Jewish image of a blessing. In many ways it is also the Jewish image of life.

The purpose of blessings is to call our attention to spiritually dramatic moments and experiences that often get overlooked. When one sees a flash of lightning illuminate the sky, the blessing to be recited is; *Blessed are You God, Sovereign of the universe, Who constantly renews creation*. Blessings are tools designed to enable us to truly *see* the wonders that are all around us.

At the same time, however, we don't have blessings for most of what we do in life. There is no blessing before you work in your garden, buy a card for an ailing friend, make lunch for your kids or put your glasses on (although there is one for putting your shoes on).

The blessings that we do say are there to sensitize us to the fact that much of what we do is a blessing. In being directed to say some blessings, we are being guided to notice all blessings. In this respect, Chanukah is like a blessing.

"These lights—they are holy; and we are not permitted to use them: Rather only to look at them." There is wonder in much that we do and see but never take note of. Much of what seems to be commonplace, pedestrian and drab actually contains sparks of life, of light and of holiness. For eight days we are merely asked to look at the simple lights of the menorah.

And what do we see? Small flames that we've seen a thousand times before? Just another colored candle? An insignificant source of light? Or is there more? Can we look beyond the little flames. Can we see to the time when Jew struggled against Greek? Can we see the spiritual strength of our people, a small flask of oil burning for eight days, a miracle, a wonder, a light. Can we possibly see all of this and more in the lights of the menorah? Our tradition tells us that on Chanukah, all we should do is look. And if we look we will see, and if we can see we will be lifted and inspired. And if on Chanukah we are able to see, who knows, we just might discover that there is much more to behold in life than we ever realized. More blessing, more life and more light.

(III)

JEWISH WOMEN, JEWISH HISTORY AND CHANUKAH

Harvard University recently received a three million dollar grant to establish a chair in Holocaust studies. The prospect of establishing such a chair has sparked controversy over whether or not such a chair is appropriate at all. Many people feel that an overemphasis on the Holocaust in particular, and the persecution of Jews in general, tends to overshadow a far more significant dimension of Jewish history: the survival of the Jewish people and their religion despite the historical forces allied against them.

Against impossible odds, the Jewish people carried their Torah across the countries and rebuilt a sovereign state in Israel. Harvard would do well to remember that the story of Jewish tragedy has a powerful counterpoint in the story of Jewish triumph.

Jonathan Mahler, New York Times Op-Ed Page

The story of the Jewish people is the story of Jewish continuity. Jewish history is the account of the Jews' ability to successfully transmit a living tradition of values, beliefs, practices, morality and spirituality from one generation to the next. An overview of the formative stages of the Jewish people together with the central themes of almost every holiday that relates to the Jews as a nation reveals the prominent, if not dominant, role of Jewish women and their uniquely feminine sensitivity, insight and spirituality in the Jewish people's ability to survive and thrive from one generation to the next for over three thousand years. Let's take a look.

ABRAHAM AND SARAH

Abraham was the first person to recognize the existence of God and to reject paganism. Abraham, together with his wife, Sarah, built the first Jewish family—though they were not "one big happy family." Abraham and Sarah had two sons, Isaac and Yishmael. The boys didn't get along very well and their relationship was the cause of a lot of parental anguish and tension. Abraham and Sarah had very different approaches to parenting. In the end, God Himself had some advice for Abraham:

> *And God said to Abraham . . . "Whatever Sarah says to you, listen to her voice . . ."*
>
> Genesis 21:12

ISAAC AND REBECCAH

Isaac and Rebeccah were the second Jewish family and they continued along the path blazed by Abraham and Sarah: One God, no praying to idols or crocodile deities and a moral and spiritual way of life that flowed from their relationship with God. But they too faced great challenges in raising their children. Their two sons, Jacob and Esau, were a study in contrasts. You know how it is; one always did his homework when he got home and the other was a Nintendo addict. Again, the parents couldn't agree on how to raise their children. Rebeccah, however, was confident that she, like Sarah before her, knew what was best for the family and took matters into her own hands.

> *"And now my son [said Rebeccah to Jacob] listen to my voice and do what I say"* . . . *And Jacob said to Rebeccah his mother ". . . what if my father figures out what's going on . . ." And she said, "my son, just listen to my voice."*

> Genesis 27:8-13

EGYPT AND PASSOVER

Sarah was right about her children, Rebeccah was right about hers and their insights and efforts paid off in the third-generation Jewish family. The children of Jacob, Rachel and Leah—though they went through a very contentious time—eventually overcoming their differences and becoming a close family unit. While internally they did live "happily ever after," external forces soon conspired to place them and their children in dire circumstances.

The descendants of Abraham, Sarah, Isaac, Rebeccah, Jacob, Rachel and Leah soon found themselves enslaved at the hands of the cruel Egyptians. And what was their response to slavery? The Jews in Egypt gave in to despair, lost their will to resist and gave up all hope in the future—at least the Jewish men did. Listen to what our tradition says.

Pharaohs decree to kill all baby boys was so devastating that the Jewish men in Egypt decided that they would have no more children. How could one bring children into such a harsh and cruel world?

> *But a young girl named Miriam protested and said to her father, "You are more cruel than Pharaoh. His decree is*

against the boys but your decree is also against the girls."
Miriam's father, Amram, could not argue with his
daughter. Eventually Amram and Yocheved gave birth to a
boy named Moses, the future savior and leader of the Jewish
people.

Talmud

And the king of Egypt said to the Jewish midwives . . . "if
it is a boy, you must kill him, but if it is a girl, you can let
her live." But the midwives were aware of God and they did
not do as they were ordered . . . and they were summoned
by the king.

Exodus 1:15-21

Can you imagine the courage of those midwives? They too
were tired, hungry and seemingly broken slaves, yet they had
the strength to defy Pharaoh.

It was in the merit of the righteous women that the Jewish
people were liberated from slavery in Egypt.

Talmud

The holiday of Passover celebrates the exodus from Egypt
and the birth of the Jewish nation. Had it not been for the
commitment and strength of the Jewish women, there would be
no Passover and no Jewish people.

THE TORAH, SHAVUOT AND RUTH

The Jewish people made it out of infancy, thanks to Sarah
and Rebeccah; grew into a nation, thanks to the women in
Egypt; and then traveled to the foot of Mount Sinai where God
gave them the Torah.

*And God called to him [Moses] from the mountain, saying,
'This is what you should say to the House of Jacob and tell
the Children of Israel.*

Exodus 19:3

*When the Torah says, "House of Jacob" this is referring to
the women, and when it says "Children of Israel" this
means the men.*

Midrash

Our tradition tells us that when God instructed Moses to
present the Torah to the Jewish people, first it was to be offered
to the women (the House of Jacob) and only then was it to be
presented to the men (the Children of Israel). Our sages further
explain that the reason the Torah was first presented to the
women was because it would primarily be their responsibility to
mold children and families that would be hospitable to the Torah
and its wisdom, ethics, values and way of life. In effect, God was
telling Moses that if the women were not prepared to accept the
Torah, then he shouldn't even bother offering it to the men.

Now let's take another look at the verse above from the
book of Exodus. What is apparent is that not only was the Torah
first offered to the Jewish women, as our sages point out, but
also that the Torah was offered in the context of families: to the
"House of Jacob" and the "Children of Israel." When God gave
the Torah to the Jewish people, He was in essence giving it to
Jewish families. And in giving the Torah to Jewish families, God
was entrusting it first and foremost to Jewish women.

*What families have in common around the world is that
they are the place where people learn who they are and how
to be that way.*

Jean Illsley Clarke, *Self-Esteem*

There is a prevailing misconception that the synagogue is the focus of Judaism. On the contrary, the center of Jewish life, the strongest formative Jewish influence . . . and the bastion of Jewish survival for so many centuries of exile have been the home and the family.

Shoshana Pantel Zolty, *And All Your Children Shall Be Learned*

My son, heed your father's guidance, and do not abandon the Torah of your mother.

King Solomon, Proverbs

Four centuries after the Torah was given to the Jewish people, King Solomon made a point of highlighting a critical aspect of Jewish continuity. Yes, both parents are vital to the educational process of their children; however, King Solomon emphasized, in some way a child's most fundamental connection to the Torah—to Judaism—is instilled not by the father, not by the synagogue Rabbi or classroom teacher, but by the special communicative abilities of a mother.

So there you have it. Not only did the women get the Jewish people out of Egypt, but they were also the indispensable factor that enabled the Jews to receive the Torah. Therefore, it should come as no surprise that on Shavuot, the holiday that celebrates the giving of the Torah, the book that is read in synagogue to reinforce the themes of the holiday is a book about a woman and her commitment to Judaism and the Jewish people: the Book of Ruth. Ruth is the paradigm for everything that Shavuot represents: commitment to the Torah and Judaism, to family and ultimately to the eternity of the Jewish people.

TROUBLE IN THE DESERT

SCENE I

Three million Jews are standing at the foot of Mount Sinai. It has been about two months since ten of the most mind-blowing plagues anyone ever saw were used to liberate them from slavery. And now God Himself is speaking from the heavens above Sinai. The entire Jewish nation has agreed to accept the Torah, and Moses is headed to the top of the mountain where he will be given two tablets with ten world-shaping commandments on them.

And then what happens? Moses doesn't come down from the mountain exactly when the Jewish people expect him to, and they become so upset they build a golden calf to worship. Our tradition tells us, however, that two groups of Jews refused to participate in the fiasco of the golden calf. One was the tribe of Levi. And the other? The women, of course.

SCENE II

Later, the same Jewish people who had been liberated from slavery in Egypt, who saw the Red Sea split to let them cross, who received the Torah at Mount Sinai and who survived the golden calf scandal are camped at the border of Israel, about to enter the Promised Land. Listen to what happened:

Moses decides to send a band of spies to scout out the land before the Jewish people enter. When the spies return they report that:

> *The nation that lives in Israel is a fearsome one, and their cities are well fortified . . . we'll never be able to take that land, they are just too strong . . . when we looked at them we felt like little grasshoppers and that's how they looked at us too.*

Numbers 13:28-33

That night (after hearing the report of the spies) the people wept. And they said to Moses, "Why did God bring us here just to die? Wouldn't we be better off if we went back to Egypt?" So they said to one another, "Let's appoint another leader and go back to Egypt."

Numbers 14:1-4

As you can imagine, both Moses and God were very disappointed in the spies and in the reaction of the people. Nobody ever said this Chosen People stuff was going to be easy, but God had hoped that after all they had been through the Jews would trust Him and would be confident that, one way or another, He would get them into the Promised Land. But that's not what happened. As a result, God decided that the people weren't yet ready to enter the land of Israel and that they needed to wander in the desert for forty years until the older generation died off and a younger generation could take their place—with one exception.

The women who heard the report of the spies did not die during the forty years in the desert because they had a deep love for the land of Israel. The men said, "Let's go back to Egypt' but the women said 'No, we were promised that land and we should just go claim our inheritance."

Midrash

THE STORY OF PURIM

Two major Jewish holidays came into being long after the Torah was given. One is Purim and the other is Chanukah.

Purim celebrates the salvation of the Jewish people from vicious Persian anti-Semitism that had been stirred up by an evil man named Haman. Haman convinced the Persian king that it was in his best interest to implement a final solution for his Jewish population. The king issued a decree stating that on a particular day, all Jews were fair game and anyone who wished could participate in the slaughter of the Jews. The Persian police would look the other way.

Thanks to the heroic efforts of a sage named Mordecai and a Jewish woman named Esther, Haman's scheme was eventually thwarted.

Esther stands for all time as the symbol of a person prepared to sacrifice everything—wealth, position, power and even life itself—for the sake of her people. Every year when we celebrate Purim, one of the primary observances of the holiday is to attend synagogue twice (once at night and again in the morning) to hear the reading of: The Book of Esther.

THE STORY OF CHANUKAH

One of the central themes in the story of Chanukah is the dedication and heroism of Jewish women.

I. YEHUDIS AND THE DECREES

The Greek rulers of Israel instituted two decrees.

Decree 1. All brides were required to sleep with a Greek military officer before they could marry their husbands.

This is not a myth or a fairy tale. These were young Jewish women who were as alive, intelligent and talented as any Jewish woman today. They were in love with their soon-to-be husbands and each had to submit herself to the lusts of a Greek soldier before she could marry. Defy the law, and she could be killed. What would you do in such a circumstance? What would you tell your daughter to do, or your fiancée?

Some Jewish women decided not to marry rather than submit to rape, while others planned clandestine marriages. The fortunate ones escaped the decree, others were killed for their defiance and many others still were ravaged by Greek officers. Whatever a woman chose, her choice was a heroic act of defiance that was driven by her commitment to Judaism and the Jewish people. Allow Jewish women to become wholesale prey for the Greek officers? Never! So they surrendered their right to marry rather than surrender the dignity of Jewish women. Plan a clandestine wedding at the risk of death? Is not the continuation of a new generation of Jewish homes and families worth the ultimate risk? Try to imagine the heart-breaking and life threatening dilemmas faced by Jewish women of the Chanukah era. Think about the statements made by their choices.

There is a story about a Jewish woman named Yehudis that has become an integral part of the psyche of Chanukah. This is her story:

A Greek commander led his army to put down a revolt that was beginning in Jerusalem. The Greek forces encamped around the walls of the city and began a protracted siege. Though Jerusalem was a well-fortified city, the relentless siege by a superior army began to exact a great toll on the citizens of the city. A widow named Yehudis left the city and requested an audience with the commander. Her plan was to seduce him and then to kill him; and her plan succeeded. The commander gave a feast in honor of Yehudis and he became quite drunk. That night the commander and Yehudis retired to his private tent where he soon fell into a deep sleep. While he was asleep Yehudis took his sword, and decapitated him. Yehudis then brought the commanders head back to Jerusalem where it was hung on the walls of the city for everyone to see. The Jews were inspired by the daring heroism of Yehudis, and the Greek forces retreated. This act is seen as a turning point in the nascent revolt of the Jews against the Greeks.

Decree 2. Circumcision (*bris mila*) of newborn baby boys was declared a capital crime.

Again, put yourself in the place of the Jewish women of the time. Having gone through the agonizing trial of marriage, you now had to fear that if you had a son and if you went ahead with his circumcision, you were risking a potential death sentence.

Circumcision is the symbol of the relationship between God and the Jewish people. Even today it is widely practiced even by Jews who retain little if any other vestige of Jewish practice. Would you allow your son to be circumcised at the risk of his life and yours? Would you advise your daughter to have a bris for her son under such circumstances? Can you imagine the look in a woman's eyes who is nursing and comforting her baby moments after his bris only to be discovered by Greek soldiers searching for just this kind of violation? One could certainly excuse the women of the day if they refused the circumcision or perhaps tried to delay it until the situation improved. But that is not what happened. Knowing full well the risks involved, Jewish women insisted that their young sons be properly brought into the nation of Israel.

One morning in Janowska, I was standing and sawing wood with another inmate of the Janowska Road Camp. To humiliate us as much as possible, I was assigned a sawing partner who was much shorter than I am. This made our sawing not only difficult but a laughable sight to watch. And the Germans found great delight in our misery and suffering.

One morning, on Hoshanah Rabbah (the last day of Sukkot), as we were sawing wood, the wind carried in our direction piercing, tormented cries like I had never heard before. I heard another worker say, "It's a children's aktion (round-up), little angels from the district are being brought to meet their maker." As we continued sawing the wood, our eyes became heavier and heavier with tears.

Suddenly I heard the voice of a woman. "Jews, have mercy on me and give me a knife." Her eyes were on fire and I knew she wanted to commit suicide. "Why are you in such a rush to get to the world of truth? We will get there sooner or later, what difference does a day make?" Suddenly a German soldier appeared, "What does she want?" He demanded. "She asked for a knife and I explained to her that we Jews are not permitted to take our lives; our lives belong to God."

The woman noticed the outline of a knife in the soldier's shirt pocket. In a strong German voice she commanded, "Give me that pocket knife." The stunned German handed her the knife. The woman bent down and picked up a bundle of rags. She unwrapped the bundle and uncovered a newborn baby sleeping on a clean white pillow. In a clear and intense voice she recited the blessing for a circumcision and circumcised her son.

She straightened her back and looked up at the heavens, "God of the universe, you have given me a healthy child. I am returning to you a wholesome, kosher Jew." [10]

II. CHANA AND HER SONS

The story of Chana and her sons is one of the most heartrending in all of Jewish history. It is also an integral part of the Chanukah tradition. The Greeks tried in many ways to humiliate the Jews, to crush their spirits and to tear them away from Judaism.

Chanah and her seven sons were brought before king Antiochus. Antiochus fancied himself to be a deity and had statues made of himself. One by one he ordered Chanah's sons to acknowledge his godliness by bowing down to an idol of himself. The first son, the oldest, refused to bow down and acknowledge any power other than that of God. For his refusal he was slowly and brutally tortured in front of his mother and brothers. Then his dismembered body was cooked in a large pot. One by one each one of the brothers refused the king's command and Chana watched the butchering of her six oldest sons. Finally, when it came to her youngest son, Antiochus promised him riches and honor if he would agree to bow down, but he too refused. Giving the young child one last chance, Antiochus approached Chanah and said that as a show of mercy he would give her some time to speak to her last remaining son to persuade him to spare himself and his mother by bowing down to the statue. Chana took her son aside, kissed him gently and said, "My son, listen carefully to my words: I carried you for nine months, nursed you for two years and have fed and cared for you up to this very day. To the best of my ability I have taught you about God and the Torah. Do not exchange your commitment and loyalty to Judaism for the fleeting offerings of a king who will soon perish himself . . ." With that, Chana watched her seventh son go to his death.

Chana stood by the heaped bodies of her sons. She prayed for them, for the Jewish people and to be taken by God rather than be killed by the Greeks. As she finished her prayer, she breathed her last breath and fell dead beside her children.

The miracle and salvation of Chanukah was a result of the actions of Jewish women. Therefore, for at least a half hour after the flames of the menorah are kindled, women should not engage in work.

The Laws of Chanukah

(IV)

Get Up, Go to Work, Come Home, Watch TV, Go to Sleep, Get Up, Go to Work . . .

One should not kindle the Chanukah lights before the sun has finished setting and should be careful that there is enough oil to last until there are no more feet in the marketplace.

Shulchan Aruch, Code of Jewish Living

I want you to carefully read the above quote because you are about to be tested on your knowledge of Jewish law. You will have two questions plus a bonus question. (Don't be nervous; it's a multiple-choice test.)

Question 1: According to the Code of Jewish Living, what is the earliest time one can light the menorah?
(A) Six-thirty eastern standard time.
(B) As soon as the sun has set.
(C) Whatever time most people come home from work.
(D) The time when the sky begins to darken.

Question 2: According to the Code of Jewish Living, until what time at night are the lights of your menorah supposed to stay lit?
(A) Until the night sky is filled with stars.
(B) Until a half-hour after sunset.
(C) Until nine o'clock Monday thorough Friday and six o'clock on the weekend.
(D) Until all the stores in your neighborhood are closed.

Answers: #1 (B) #2 (B)

Bonus Question: If the correct answer to question 2 is (B)—that your menorah only has to stay lit until a half-hour after sunset—then why doesn't the Code of Jewish Living just say "be careful that there is enough oil to last for half an hour" instead of using the ambiguous statement of "until there are no more feet in the market-place"?

When we look at the phrase "until there are no more feet in the marketplace" in Hebrew, we discover something very interesting. The Hebrew word for "no more," *tichle*, also means eradicate, and the Hebrew word for "feet," *regel*, is also the root of the Hebrew word for "routine," *regelut*. With this in mind, we can now read the phrase as follows: "be careful that there is enough oil to last until the routine caused by the marketplace has been eradicated." What we have discovered is that hidden within the words that tell us how long our menorahs need to burn is an allusion to another spiritual dimension of Chanukah.

Until the routine caused by the marketplace has been eradicated. The marketplace is where the rhythm of everyday living is transformed into the repetitive cadence of routine and monotony. We get up, read the paper, go to work, have lunch, go back to work, go home, run to the dry cleaner, the supermarket and the video store, watch television, go to sleep, get up, read the paper and go to work; over and over and over again until our lives become little more than moving from one all-too-familiar routine to the next. And then comes Chanukah and the lighting of the menorah.

> **The dancing flames of the menorah are there to spark a sense of innovation in life.**

Within the lights of the Chanukah menorah is a spiritual energy that is able to help us reconnect with that which is inspiring and uplifting in life. Chanukah is a time for innovation. It is a time to break free of routine and introduce a sense of freshness into life. But how can we do this? The answer is one part effort and one part inspiration from above.

The effort required on Chanukah involves putting aside some time to recall those moments in life when you felt inspired and uplifted, when you felt connected to a larger sense of reality that transcended yourself. When was the last time you felt that being alive was awe-inspiring and not boring? When was the last time you felt a sense of odyssey in life? When was the last time you felt your soul to be the most powerful force in your life? When was the last time you were aware of the presence of God?

The "marketplace" has an insidious way of replacing that which is able to illuminate our lives with the hazy clouds of routine. Chanukah is a time of war and the battlefront is the marketplace. When, during Chanukah, one strives to reconnect with even one thing that can provide a deep sense of meaning, inspiration and aliveness, then the power of the Chanukah lights can step in and do its part. As we seek inspiration, we will be inspired. As we reach for meaning, we will find that opportunities are right in front of us; and as we yearn to dispel the darkness bred by routine, we will discover that we are surrounded by sources of light that are just waiting for us to reach out and grasp them.

(V)

COMPETITION

OF WINNERS AND LOSERS

Com´pe·ti´tion 1. the act of competing; rivalry. 2. a contest in which a winner is selected from among two or more entrants.

I was competitive in everything I did—sports, schoolwork, everything. You have to be a competitor. You can't be soft. You have to want the best.

Jack Nicklaus

While the law of competition may be sometimes hard for the individual, it is best for the race, because it insures the survival of the fittest in every department.

Andrew Carnegie

I'm obsessed with winning . . . That's what this country's all about.

George Steinbrenner, business executive,
New York Yankees owner

The aim of all competition is victory, to vanquish one's rivals and to come out on top. The greatest value, and arguably the only value, in a competitive environment is winning. Competition by definition is the endeavor that produces, out of a field of participants, only one winner. Interestingly, in the Greek Olympic games there was only one "place"—first place. The other contestants, whether they came in second or thirty-second—and even if they did their absolute best—were all losers. In competition, results are paramount, and all results are measured by stacking them up against those of other people. In other words, competition allows for the existence of only two types of people: winners and losers. And generally, the losers far outnumber the winners.

We try to be good parents and to tell our children "It doesn't matter whether you win or lose, it's how you play the game," but they find out soon enough (usually from us) that that's just not the way the world works. It does matter if you win or lose. It matters in school, in getting accepted to the right university; it matters at the office, in your career and certainly in business. Winning is everything.

PRECIOUS LIGHTS

Our ancient tradition tells us of a fascinating exchange between God and the Jewish people. This is how the conversation went:

Jewish Nation: *God, You illuminate the whole world and then tell us to light the menorah?*

God: *The little lights of your menorah are more precious to me than the lights of all the stars I have placed in the sky.*

The Chanukah menorah is meant to be a spiritual counter-weight to the competitive notion of measuring success only by beating someone else and focusing only on results to the exclusion of effort and growth. Judaism says that the world can be a place where everyone is a winner. That each and every individual and each and every family is capable of being a unique and precious source of light. When the Jewish people engaged God in dialogue they wanted to know, How can our candles, our little menorahs, possibly compete with the stars that fill the heavens? Can our little lights possibly add any light to a world illuminated by the sun, a universe blanketed with billions of stars?

In the realm of the soul, in the realm of deepest human accomplishment, there is no room for competition, yet room enough for a world full of precious little lights.

The answer of course, is no. There is no way that our little menorahs can possibly compete with the light of all those stars. And that's just the point.

To be a star, a brilliant source of light, you don't have to be brighter than any other stars. To be good does not mean that you have to be better than anyone else. To be wise does not mean that you have to be the wisest of all people. To be kind does not mean that you have to be the kindest person anyone has ever met, and to be holy, to soar spiritually, does not mean that you have to be the holiest person of all.

Each and every one of us is a precious source of light, and when God told us that the little lights of the menorah are more precious than the stars in the sky, He was telling us not to evaluate the beauty and radiance of our inner lights in terms of anything else but ourselves. In the realm of spirituality and true human accomplishment, there is no room for competition, yet room enough for a world full of winners—a world full of precious little lights.

FAMILY LIGHTS

Competition puts us in the habit of assessing the value of something or someone by comparing it to something else. In the realm of family dynamics this can be a very destructive tendency. A husband who feels that his wife is always comparing his career, his status and the size of his paycheck with those of other men will become quite resentful. Similarly, a woman who feels that her husband is comparing her career, cooking or child-rearing skills with those of other women will also become very resentful. And perhaps worst of all, those children who feel that their parents want them to be everything they aren't, but everything their friends' children are, will be deprived of the chance to develop a sense of self-worth.

Chanukah is the ideal time for families to put aside habits of comparing and to focus on the beauty inherent in one another. Try thinking of your family members as menorahs, and each night make it your business to notice and to light another flame. Here is one way to do this.

Before Chanukah buy a special notebook that will be known as your "family lights notebook." Divide this notebook into sections with one section for each member of the family. Each night of Chanukah, before you light your menorahs, give everyone in the family one sheet of paper for each member of the family. On that piece of paper each person will write a response to one of the following statements.

1. You bring light into my life when you _____.
2. I love the way you _____.
3. Whenever I see you _____ , it reminds me how special you are.
4. You make our family special because you _____.

Each night of Chanukah these "pages of light" will be added to each person's section in the family notebook. By the eighth night of Chanukah, as the flames of your menorah burn bright, the precious flames of your family will also be burning a little brighter.

(VI)

DAYS OF EIGHT

Have you ever sensed that there is more to life than you can touch or feel or smell? That there is a dimension to reality that cannot be experienced by any of your senses but that you know to be as real as the feeling you have when holding the hand of someone you love? Are you convinced that you have a soul, a nonphysical core to your being that will never be detected by an x-ray, MRI or any other type of technology? Do you believe in God?

If you answered yes to any of these questions, then Chanukah is the holiday for you.

The world was created in seven days and therefore, in Jewish thought, the number seven represents the natural, physical world, the world that we can touch and smell and feel. The number eight, on the other hand, represents that which transcends the natural world, that which emanates from beyond the limits of our senses but which we feel we can reach out and touch—and be touched by and stirred by.

The Greeks had a particular dislike of the Jewish practice of *bris mila*, the circumcision of a baby boy on the eighth day after his birth. First of all it offended their ideas of beauty and the emphasis on perfecting the human body. Public nudity was not uncommon in Greek society because the body was seen as just another form of art. A beautifully developed body was no less an esthetic accomplishment than a beautiful sculpture or a beautiful building. What's more, because man was seen as the noblest of all creatures, a perfectly sculpted body was arguably the finest conceivable work of art. To the Greeks a bris mila was no less than than the mutilation of a masterpiece—it was like spray painting a Renoir.

During the period of Greek oppression, one of the primary targets of the Greeks was bris mila. The observance of Shabbat, the declaration of each new month, the study of Torah and bris mila all became capital offenses.

Bris mila makes the following statement: The human body, and the human being, can only achieve its greatest beauty if it is affected by a relationship with God. The perfectly sculpted life is a life that recognizes and embraces the spiritual essence of reality. Such a view of life flew in the face of the highest Greek ideals, namely, that ultimate beauty and perfection issue from the hands and the mind of man working in concert with nature. The Jewish view is that ultimate beauty and virtue lie in the hands of man only when he reaches up and grasps that which transcends the natural world.

> *The Greeks gathered against me; then in the days of the Hasmoneans. They breached the walls of my towers; and defiled all the oils. And from the one remaining flask a miracle occurred. The wise sages, days of eight they proclaimed for song and rejoicing.*
>
> Ma'otsur, Rock of Salvation (sung nightly after lighting the menorah)

Everyone knows that Chanukah is eight days long because the miracle of the oil lasted for eight days. However, in the traditional ma'otsur song we find a very curious phrase: "The wise sages, days of eight they proclaimed for song and rejoicing." It doesn't say that they proclaimed that there be an eight-day holiday but rather they proclaimed a holiday that was "days of eight."

The eight days of Chanukah are *days of eight*. Days of transcendence. Days of opportunity to look both within ourselves and beyond ourselves, and to sense that there is far more to our existence than the world of nature could ever contain.

The Greeks detested bris mila because of its "eightness," because it stands for transcendence. The miracle of the oil lasted for eight days as a reminder that the Jewish people, and Jewish life, are hewn from the stone of transcendence; and every day of Chanukah is a *day of eight*, a day that calls on us to join the transcendent with the worldly, the profound with the mundane, the spiritual with the physical.

(VII)

MONEY, MONEY, MONEY AND CHANUKAH

JACOB AND THE JARS

Though the events of Chanukah took place hundreds of years after the Torah was given, according to our tradition, an event recorded in the Torah foreshadowed the miracle of the oil.

Let's take a quick look at one event in the life of Jacob.

In the formative years of Jewish history, Abraham and Sarah had a son named Isaac, Isaac and Rebecca had a son named Jacob, and Jacob had a bully for a brother whose name was Esau. Eventually the situation became so bad at home that Jacob had to run away from his brother, who wanted to kill him. Years later, Esau and his thugs finally caught up with Jacob and his family. During the night before their fateful reunion, Jacob quietly moved his entire family across the river near where they had camped. Then, after having moved everyone to safety, Jacob went back to the other side of the river.

Jacob went back to the other side because he forgot some small jars. "Therefore," said God,"because you took the risk

*of going back for a few jars, I will repay your children with
a small jar that will be found by the Maccabees."*

Midrashic Tradition

*Jacob went back to the other side because he forgot some
small jars. This teaches us that the righteous care more
about their money than their own lives.*

Talmud

Think about this for a minute. Jacob goes back to retrieve some small jars and somehow that act is so significant that it enables his descendents, over a thousand years later, to find the one remaining jar of oil not defiled by the Greeks? The jar of oil that would be the source of the Chanukah miracle? Additionally, we are also supposed to learn from this very same episode how important money is to righteous people? There is more to this puzzle.

*There is an ancient custom to give children money, known
as Chanukah gelt, on Chanukah.*

Jewish custom

*It is forbidden to derive any benefit from the lights of the
Chanukah menorah ... even to use the light to count your
money.*

Code of Jewish Living, The Laws of Chanukah

There seems to be some kind of a relationship between Chanukah and money. First, Chanukah is the only holiday that has a custom centered on money, the custom of Chanukah gelt. Second, when the Code of Jewish Living wants to illustrate the prohibition against deriving benefit from the menorah, the example it uses is, "even to use the light to count your money."

Think of all the examples that could have been used. The law could have said don't eat by the light of the menorah, don't write a letter by the light of the menorah, don't let your children do their homework by the light of the menorah, but of all things, it said, *don't count your money by the light of the menorah.* And then when we study the story of Jacob in the Torah and our tradition tells us that embedded in this story is a hint to the future miracle of Chanukah, we find that the very same verse that alludes to Chanukah also teaches us this curious lesson about how righteous people love money (which doesn't exactly sound like righteous behavior).

So what is it? What is this relationship between Chanukah and money?

THE HISTORY OF MONEY

It is impossible for us to imagine a world without money, but once upon a time that's the way it was. You are probably wondering, how could somebody buy a shovel in a moneyless world? Simple; all that was required was to have an extra saw at home and then to find someone with an extra shovel who just happened to need a saw. Once you located such a person you just swapped your saw for his shovel and everyone was happy. A tedious, inefficient and bothersome way to execute transactions you say. Well, now you know why money was invented. Once money was invented it was only a matter of time until a sort of monetary evolution produced a modern economy with millions of products that could be easily bought and sold.

THE CONCEPT OF MONEY

There was a time when a U.S. dollar bill was backed up by a dollar's worth of gold in Fort Knox, but that is no longer the case. Today our money is little more than a symbolic representation of value. The reason our dollar bills still have worth beyond the negligible value of the paper they're printed on is because people have agreed to willingly exchange these pieces of paper for other people's goods and services. When you think about it, however, even in earlier times when money was actual coins of gold, silver or some other precious metal, these metals also had value only because there was a general agreement that they would be treated as valuable and thus be accepted in exchange for goods.

In essence, the conceptual difference between money and actual goods is that one has intrinsic value and the other has only a representative value. A lawnmower is valuable because it performs a valuable function; it cuts grass and simplifies the life of it's owner. A bronze coin, a twenty dollar bill, a personal check or a plastic credit card derive their value not from what they are or what they do, but from the fact that they can easily be used to acquire all sorts of goods that are intrinsically valuable. You can't do much with paper money other than use it as a bookmark, but you can turn it into almost anything you desire. Money, then, represents potential.

JACOBS MONEY AND THE POTENTIAL OF CHANUKAH

As you recall, Jacob went back for some small jars and our tradition reveals two hidden meanings within that episode. First, there is the idea that those jars would somehow live again in the jar of oil found at the time of Chanukah, and second, there is the odd notion that righteous people value money more than their own well-being.

Money, as we have discovered, is actually potential. One person looks at a hundred dollar bill and sees a CD player, another sees a watch and yet another sees a bicycle for their nieces birthday. Money, in and of itself has virtually no value, but it's potential is almost limitless.

The lesson that Jacob valued money and the lesson of Chanukah are one in the same. Potential.

People look at money, but they see far more than is actually present; they see all sorts of potential. When the Jews resisted the Greeks they did so because they lived in the world of potential, a deep and often hidden world that lies beneath the surface. On the surface, it was preposterous for the Jews to resist the Greeks. Greek culture was overwhelming the world, Hellenism was the wave of the future and militarily no one could stand in the Greeks' path, certainly not a band of renegade Jews. That, however, was the view from the surface. The view through the lens of potential was far different.

The Jewish people knew that they were an eternal people. A people whose way of life and whose message of values, morality and spirituality was destined not only to last forever but also to have a world-shaping impact. This was the world of Jewish potential: a tiny and ill-equipped people was prepared to take on the superpower of its day, all because the Jews believed in the potential of Jewish destiny. They believed that no matter how dire things looked, there existed within the Jewish people, within the Jewish soul, the ability to vanquish the mightiest of foes and eventually fulfill their own mission of being, in the words of the prophet, "A light unto the nations."

The Egyptian, the Babylonian and the Persian rose, filled the planet with sound and splendor, then faded to dream-stuff and passed away. The Greek and the Roman followed and made a vast noise, and they are gone; other peoples have sprung up and held their torch high for a time, but it burned out, and they sit in twilight now, or have vanished. The Jew saw them all, beat them all, and is now what he always was; exhibiting no decadence, no infirmities of age, no weakening of his parts, no slowing of his energies, no dulling of his alert and aggressive mind. All things are mortal but the Jew; all other forces pass, but he remains.

Mark Twain

What Mark Twain understood in hindsight, the Jews at the time of Chanukah already knew because they lived not only in the world as it appeared but also in the world of potential.

When we light our menorahs we need to look closely at those tiny flames and contemplate the world of potential. Where others see darkness, we are called to see light. We need to look at our children, look beyond the problems and the quarrels, and see potential. We need to look at one another, beyond the faults and the foibles, and see potential. We need to look at life, beyond all the pain and struggles, and see potential. We need to look at our people, beyond the divisions and the hatred, and see potential. In everything we encounter, we need to look beneath the surface, to discover the soul, and to realize our ultimate potential.

LET'S DO CHANUKAH: AN OVERVIEW OF THE OBSERVANCES AND CUSTOMS OF CHANUKAH

HADLAKOT NEIROT : TO KINDLE THE MENORAH

WHAT: The primary obligation is to have at least one menorah kindled in every Jewish home on each of the eight nights of Chanukah.

HOW: 1) One should make sure that either the candles or the oil in one's menorah is sufficient to burn for at least half an hour. (Those trusty old colored candles make it in just under the wire.)

2) On the first night one candle is lit, on the second night two candles are lit and so on until all eight are lit on the last night of Chanukah.

There is an aspect of the lighting that people are often unaware of and that can be a little bit confusing. The procedure for lighting goes like this.

On the first night you light the candle on the far right-hand side of the menorah. That's easy enough; now here's the tricky part. After the first night you add new candles for the subsequent nights from right to left; however, you light them moving from left to right. Let's take night three as an example.

Night three: Candle number one (color is irrelevant) is placed in the holder to your far right, candle number two is placed in the holder immediately to the left of candle number one, and candle number three is placed immediately to the left of candle number two. Now that you've lined them up properly, it's time to switch directions for the actual lighting. The first candle you light is the one to your far left, and then moving to your right you light the other candles, always ending with the one to your extreme right.

(IMPORTANT: Do not confuse your *shamesh* with candle number one. The word *shamesh* means "helper" and that is exactly what it is. It helps you light the other candles, but it is not counted among the actual lights of Chanukah. As a rule, menorahs are made in such a way that the *shamesh* is set slightly apart from the other candles. This is done to clearly distinguish the *shamesh* from the other "mitzvah candles.")

WHEN: The ideal time for lighting the menorah is just after nightfall. However, one can light the menorah anytime during the night. If Mom or Dad won't be home from work until late, it is certainly appropriate to wait until the whole family can be together to light the menorah.

WHY: The procedure for kindling the flames of the menorah is representative of a well-traveled pathway in spiritual growth.

THE CANDLE AND THE SOUL

For God's candle is the soul of Man.

Proverbs

The flames of the menorah are small and silent.

On the first night of Chanukah we light one candle, one flame. Small and silent. We walk into the room and we barely notice its presence. It's there but it's very subtle. Like our souls, the flame is there but it is very, very subtle.

As we hurtle through a thousand things that fill our days with noise and confusion and countless loose ends, it's very easy to lose track of our souls. There's just too much going on. There are family obligations, kids, school, the office, dating, vacations, the six o'clock news, the fortunes of our favorite teams, making dinner, reading our E-mail, getting the car fixed, returning overdue books, returning calls, paying the bills and surfing the Web. And amidst all of this we're supposed to remember that each of us has a soul? That deep down there is an inner essence that also wants and needs a bit of attention? That there is a part of us that wants to do more than tasks and errands; that longs to touch a bit of the infinite, the luminous, the precious and the divine in our lives? But how?

The answer is by taking one small spiritual step at a time. The answer can be found in lighting the Chanukah menorah. Each night of lighting is an opportunity to nurture our souls by introducing an element of inspiration into our lives. The flames we light on the menorah possess the ability to resonate with our own inner flames—to kindle and fan the flames of our souls.

We know that life makes all sorts of demands on us, but deep down, we all sense that there are certain intangibles that represent the essence, the soul of our lives. The lighting of the menorah creates a new space in our lives. A space where we can, for a while, divest ourselves of everything else that tugs at us and focus on the "deep down" of life. Who we truly are—deep down. Who we want to be—deep down. What we want to do with this brief time we call life, what we want to stand for and what we want to do—*deep down*.

YOUR INNER FLAME

Here is one approach to accessing your inner flame.

Each night of Chanukah take some time to reflect on one of the following issues. You may find it especially helpful to create a Chanukah journal to record your thoughts and reflections. (Space has been provided on page 153 to write your reflections.)

1) "Deep down, what I truly want is _____."
2) "I feel most in touch with my soul when _____."
3) "What can I do tomorrow that will in some way express the deepest part of who I am?"
4) If you could give yourself just one piece of advice for keeping in touch with your deepest aspirations, what would you say?
5) If you could give your spouse, child or best friend just one tip for not losing sight of the most important things in life, what would you say?

The aim of this period of reflection is to get in touch with what you truly want, what about your inner self you deem to be precious and what you long for, deep down.

Each night of Chanukah try to ponder these *deep down* issues and questions. Ask yourself a question and then just sit quietly in front of the silent glow of your menorah and listen for the soft sound of your own inner flame. It may take a few minutes or even longer, but be patient and wait for the answer to come. When it does, write down your answer. After the first night you will have one answer. The second night you'll have two and by the last night of Chanukah both the menorah in your home and the flame deep within your soul will be glowing a little more brightly.

SEDER HA'BRACHOT: THE BLESSINGS FOR

LIGHTING THE MENORAH

WHAT: The person who is lighting the menorah needs to say the special blessings that relate to both the menorah and the holiday before actually lighting the candles. Two blessings are said on all eight nights of Chanukah, and a third is added only on the first night.

BLESSING #1.

The Mitzvah of kindling the Menorah.
This blessing is said every night prior to lighting the menorah.

בָּרוּךְ אַתָּה יהוה אֱלֹהֵינוּ מֶלֶךְ הָעוֹלָם, אֲשֶׁר קִדְּשָׁנוּ
בְּמִצְוֹתָיו,וְצִוָּנוּ לְהַדְלִיק נֵר שֶׁל חֲנֻכָּה.

Blessed are You, Adonai our God, King of the Universe, Who has made us holy through His commandments, and has commanded us to kindle the light of Chanukah.

Baruch atah Adonai, eloheynu melech ha-olam, asher kidshanu b'mitzvotav, v'tzivanu l'hadlik ner shel Chanukah.

BLESSING #2.

The Blessing for the Miracle.
This blessing is said every night after the first blessing, also
before lighting the menorah.

בָּרוּךְ אַתָּה יהוה אֱלֹהֵינוּ מֶלֶךְ הָעוֹלָם, שֶׁעָשָׂה נִסִּים לַאֲבוֹתֵינוּ,
בַּיָּמִים הָהֵם בַּזְּמַן הַזֶּה.

**Blessed are You, Adonai our God, King of the Universe, Who
did miracles for our forefathers, in those days at this very time.**

*Baruch atah Adonai, eloheynu melech ha-olam, sheh-asa nisim
la'avotaynu, ba'yamim ha-haim ba'zman ha-zeh.*

BLESSING #3.

The Blessing of Gratitude.
This blessing is said on the first night only. It follows immediately after the second blessing and preceeds the lighting
of the menorah.

בָּרוּךְ אַתָּה יהוה אֱלֹהֵינוּ מֶלֶךְ הָעוֹלָם, שֶׁהֶחֱיָנוּ וְקִיְּמָנוּ וְהִגִּיעָנוּ
לַזְּמַן הַזֶּה.

**Blessed are You, Adonai our God, King of the Universe, Who has
kept us alive, sustained us and enabled us to arrive at this season.**

*Baruch atah Adonai, eloheynu melech ha-olam, sheh-heh-cheyanu,
v'kiy'manu, v'higianu la'zman ha-zeh.*

HOW: The procedure for lighting the menorah is as follows. The first thing you do is light the *shamesh*. Remember, the lighting of the shamesh is not a part of the actual mitzvah of lighting the menorah, and therefore no blessings precede its lighting. Once you have lit the shamesh and are holding it in your hand, it's time to say the appropriate blessings: all three blessings on the first night and only the first two on the last seven nights. Once you conclude the blessings, you light the candles in the order mentioned earlier. Don't forget: You light the one to your extreme left first and then proceed to your right.

WHEN: Say the blessings right before you light the menorah.

WHY: In Jewish life, whenever one is about to do a mitzvah, the performance of that mitzvah is preceded by a blessing. The purpose of these blessings is to focus one's mind on what is about to take place.

The word *mitzvah*, while its common translation is "commandment," also means "to bind." Mitzvot are vehicles for deepening our sense of spiritual connectedness to God and the Jewish people. We become bound up with and connected to that which transcends ourselves when we are involved in a mitzvah. The blessing that precedes a mitzvah is meant to direct our attention to the specific opportunity for connectedness that we are about to be a part of.

Baruch atah / **Blessed are You**

Blessings always begin with us personally addressing God, which is heavy stuff. As we are about to perform a mitzvah we need to be aware of the presence of intense spirituality. If standing at the ocean's edge and watching a sunset is awesome, if waking up to the first silent snowfall of winter or witnessing the birth of your own child is awesome, then being in the presence of the source of all nature is certainly awesome.

Blessings focus us on the awe present in every mitzvah.

ba'yamim ha-haim ba'zman ha-zeh / in those days at this very time

Ancient Chinese insights into the human body recently achieved the status of "mainstream medicine," and now many health plans will cover acupuncture treatments. Western medicine is just beginning to discover what other cultures have known for thousands of years: There is a profound mind-body relationship, and emotions can be stored in the body parts associated with those particular emotions.

Now let's think about time.

Time is not just something that passes by. In a sense, Judaism sees time as a living entity. Events don't just happen in time, they happen *to* time. Just as emotional trauma can later manifest itself as physical pain, seemingly isolated historical events can produce ripples that have an ongoing presence throughout time. The miraculous events of Chanukah may have happened *in those days,* but just as significantly, they also took place *at this very time.*

A skilled acupuncturist knows how to locate emotional energy stored up in another person's body. Likewise, someone who has devoted themselves to understanding and mastering the fulfillment of a mitzvah, knows how to access spiritual energies that are hidden within various times. These times are like seasons: they may not always be present, but they always come back. The mitzvah of lighting the menorah is not just a way of recalling a time gone by, it is a finely tuned technique for accessing the spiritual energy latent within that time.

THE PRAYER OF *AL HANISIM*: "FOR THE MIRACLES"

WHAT: During the daily prayers when one recites the *Amidah* (often referred to as the silent prayer), and also during *Birkat Hamazon* (the blessing after a meal), the special paragraph of *Al Hanisim* is inserted at a particular point in the prayers.

HOW: Any prayer book worth its weight in prayers should have instructions printed at the appropriate places. The best advice I can give you is to follow those instructions. If there are no instructions in your prayer book then it's time to visit your local Jewish bookstore and upgrade to a prayer book that comes complete with all the extras.

WHEN: The *Al Hanisim* prayer is added to all the daily prayer services in synagogue during Chanukah. Of course, if you're not so into synagogue, you can always say it on your own, in the comfort of your own home, any time during Chanukah. *Al Hanisim* is a great little prayer that will enhance your experience of Chanukah and is well worth trying at least once.

WHY: Anyone who has ever made it through a serious illness or has seen someone they love recover from an illness, knows what it means to be grateful for good health. Jewish wisdom relates to gratitude as one of the cornerstones of life, as a very basic and powerful feeling—and one that needs to be expressed.

THANKSGIVING

I once heard General George Schwarzkopf make the following statement. "Today there is only one superpower left. Think about what the world would be like if the last remaining superpower had been Mao's China, Hitler's Germany or

Stalin's Soviet Union. Thank God, if there is only one super-power, it's the United States of America." Personally, I think the general has a good point. As imperfect as America may be, I'm quite grateful things turned out the way they have and that we don't live in a world dominated by Fascism.

> *And they established these eight days of Chanukah to give thanks and praise to Your great name.*
>
> Prayer, Al Hanisim

The Grinch has already made it quite clear that Chanukah was never meant to be a time of gift giving. It is, however, meant to be a time of *thanks*giving. The question is, are we thankful? Are we thankful that the Jewish people were saved, that we have survived as a nation and that we are Jews today? I mean really thankful—the kind of thankful that General Schwarzkopf was talking about or the kind of thankful my best friend felt when his four-year-old daughter completed her chemotherapy treatments. Chanukah is the perfect time to think about and to express why you are grateful for being a Jew.

Here is a Chanukah exercise that can be done by individuals as well as families.
Every night after lighting the candles, ask the following question:

Why am I thankful for Being a Jew?

This is a simple but not so simple question.

Try to come up with a different answer every night of Chanukah. Write down your answers, and if you are doing this with your family, have everyone write down theirs. If everyone feels comfortable, you can share and discuss your answers. This makes for great discussion while enjoying your latkes.

An ongoing list of answers kept from year to year may just turn out to be one of the most important gifts you ever give your children or yourself.

MINHAGIM: THE CUSTOMS OF CHANUKAH

Customs are not obligations in the same way that mitzvot are. This is not meant to diminish their importance because they do add a great deal of spiritual spice to the main course of the holidays; however, there is a qualitative difference between a custom, such as the dreidel or latkes, and the requirement to light the menorah. If you don't light the menorah then you miss out on the essence of Chanukah, but if you don't eat any latkes or spin any dreidels you have not omitted anything essential to the holiday.

1) A Special Holiday Meal.
Unlike other holidays, there is no requirement to have a special meal on Chanukah. There is, however, a custom to add some embellishment to meals during Chanukah and to imbue these meals with a festive atmosphere. Even if one does make a festive Chanukah meal, no special blessings over wine need to be recited. It is appropriate to use these meals as a time to study about Chanukah in order to deepen one's appreciation of the entire experience.

2) Latkes (my all-time favorite custom).
The miracle of Chanukah centered around the oil that burned for eight days. For this reason it is customary to prepare foods that are fried in oil; hence, the latke. In Israel today, the latke has run into some stiff competition. *Sufganiyot*, fried jelly-filled donuts, have captured a large segment of the Chanukah market.

3) Chanukah Gelt: The Gift of Chanukah Money.

This is the closest thing you'll find to the modern-day Chanukah present. The struggle against the Greeks was a struggle to preserve the Torah. As was mentioned earlier, many teachers and their students were imprisoned or tortured for the crime of studying the Torah or were forced into hiding to continue their studies clandestinely. For this reason it became customary for the leadership of Jewish communities to focus on the financial needs of Jewish educational institutions during the time of Chanukah.

Parents would give a gift of money to their children as a reward for their involvement in Torah study. This was not meant as payment for their studies, but rather as a tangible display of parental pride in their children who continued to study the Torah that so many sacrificed so much for.

4) The Dreidel.

The game of dreidel is a centuries-old custom that is also related to the theme of Torah study. On Chanukah parents would give their children a dreidel to play with and tell them, "Play, relax and enjoy your Chanukah evenings so that you will feel refreshed and able to return to your Torah studies with new vigor."

On Chanukah we subtly teach our children that time is a precious commodity. Time is not something to be killed or taken for granted. Just the opposite, it is a vessel waiting to be filled with life. And so we tell our children—and ourselves as well—"play, relax, have fun and enjoy yourself,"—but don't consider that time as dead time or time off from life; rather, see it as an opportunity to refresh your spirit, to clear your mind and to drain away built-up tensions so that you may re-engage the pursuit of your goals with fresh vitality, energy and commitment.

SENSITIVITY TO THE VALUE OF TIME IS ONE OF THE CORNERSTONES
OF THE JEWISH APPROACH TO LIFE.

*The great rule of moral conduct is, next to God, to respect
time.*

Johann Casper Lavater

How many times have you said to yourself, "There are so
many things I'd like to do, but I just can't seem to find the time."
We all feel that way. The Jewish approach to "finding time" is to
create beachheads. This means not only being aware of the large
chunks of committed time that already fill our schedules, but
also searching out those times when we're not doing much
other than just passing time—or killing it. Then, having located
these little islands of time, we need to look for creative ways to
fill even these small amounts of time with things we "just can't
seem to find the time to do."

Many people would love to find out what's in the Torah or
know more about Judaism, but they feel overwhelmed by how
much there is to learn and how much time it will involve. The
result is that many of us never get started at all. In response to
this natural all-or-nothing tendency, Jewish consciousness
emphasizes the need to spend at least a little time every day
studying the wisdom of the Torah. In this regard it is important
to know that Jewish thought puts less emphasis on knowing
every portion of the Torah than it does on spending a portion of
every day delving into the wisdom of the Torah.

Chanukah nights are ideal for creating little beachheads in
time. After the menorah has been lit and the latkes have been
enjoyed, there is still plenty of time left in the evening. Try this:
for just ten minutes don't turn on the television, don't pick up
the paper, and don't dive back into the work you brought home

from the office. Instead, try putting aside ten minutes every night of Chanukah to read something about Judaism that you have always been curious about but never had the time to study. Who knows? That little eight-night beachhead may turn out to be a great discovery of time, knowledge and wisdom. Just think: by finding ten minutes a night you are potentially discovering over fifty hours a year. Keep that up for a few years and before long you'll know many of the things you always wanted to know and will possess more of your heritage to pass on to your children. This Chanukah you can give yourself and your family a gift more valuable than anything you'll ever find in the local mall: the gift of time.

> *Do not say "when I have the time then I'll study," because you may never find the time.*
>
> Talmud

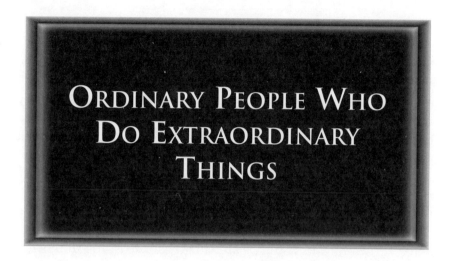

ORDINARY PEOPLE WHO
DO EXTRAORDINARY
THINGS

MESIRAT NEFESH: TRANSCENDING LIMITATIONS

Imagine that we have a time machine and can travel with the Joint Chiefs of Staff and a CNN correspondent back to the time just prior to the Jewish revolt against the Greeks.

Here's the situation: The Greek forces are the superpower of their day: well trained, equipped with the latest weaponry and battle tested—truly a first-class, professional fighting force. Facing them are the Maccabees: ill equipped, untrained and vastly outnumbered. The Maccabees have no allies—no one to supply them with any type of weapons, intelligence data or assistance of any kind.

Our CNN correspondent is now approaching the head of the Joint Chiefs of Staff. They have just completed their briefing on the situation in the Middle East.

"Excuse me, general. Could you please share your assessment of the situation with us?"

"To be perfectly honest, the Jews don't stand a chance. If they were to ask me, I'd tell them to go along with the Greeks. They can keep their religion and adopt the Greek way of life too. Look, what's so terrible about participating in some athletic competition with the Greeks? It will probably do them some good—toughen 'em up a little. And as far as those other Greek practices that the Jews find so objectionable, well, they'll just have to get used to them. I mean it's better than committing suicide, isn't it? Because that's exactly what they're going to do if they go ahead with this revolt. I say, bide your time, be reasonable, ride out the storm, and eventually the Greeks will leave you alone and you'll be able to go back to doing things the way you want to do them.

"It's either bend a little, or die. Those are the only choices the Jews have."

"Thank you, general."

"So there you have it. In the opinion of the Joint Chiefs, the Jews will either have to bend a little or die."

The general was right. The Jews didn't have a chance; however, what he didn't realize was that they also didn't have a choice. And sometimes when you know you don't have a choice, you create the possibility of a chance.

> There is an unusually potent force that is unleashed when one is confronted with a situation in which he has "no choice." In fact, this is one of the paths to realizing great spiritual heights and to achieving what a person truly wants in life.
>
> This is also the secret of the miracle of Chanukah: the victory of the "few over the many," a victory that seemed to be literally impossible. When the Hasmonean family realized that they had no choice other than to confront the Greeks and attempt the impossible, precisely at that pivotal

moment of decision they were able to link up with a force
beyond themselves and achieve the impossible. The Jewish
people reached for that which was beyond their grasp and
were thus privileged to initiate events that transcended
nature: the victory over the Greeks and the flask of oil that
burned for eight days.

Rabbi Eliyahu Dessler

The Jews who fought against the Greeks were ordinary people who were able to transcend their apparent limitations and achieve something truly extraordinary. In Jewish life this is known as *mesirat nefesh*—the willingness to offer everything you hold dear, even your very life, in the service of a greater good. Often, the only thing that separates ordinary people from extraordinary accomplishments is the realization that there is simply no other choice.

In the Jewish way of thinking most of us are pretty ordinary, yet we all possess the potential for the extraordinary. We all possess the pilot light of *mesirat nefesh*. In one way or another we are all capable of devoting that which we hold dear in the service of a goal whose value transcends ourselves.

The following stories are about ordinary people who in their own individual ways offered themselves in the service of a greater good. These stories are not about heroes who single-handedly fought off an entire batallion or who walked a hundred miles through the desert carrying a dying friend. These are stories about ordinary, everyday people who were confronted with challenges that seemed to be beyond reasonable expectations and who nonetheless offered themselves in the service of an ideal greater than themselves, and who thus became quite extraordinary.

THE SHABBOS CLUB

Eighteen years ago Rachel Schwartz and her family moved to Miami. At the same time that the Schwartzes were settling into their new home in south Florida hundreds of Russian Jewish families were also coming to the Miami area.

"One day I got a call from a teacher who worked in a new school that had a lot of Russian students. She said she felt terrible because she knew that many of these kids were living on little more than soup from week to week. She asked if I could make a shabbos dinner for a family of four, so I did."

Rachel soon realized that this family clearly needed more than just one nice Shabbos dinner. She decided to call six friends to see if each one could make dinner once a week for this Russian family. They were all glad to help out.

"I thought to myself, wow, if they're so happy to help, let me call some other people and see if they are willing to help out too. And that's how the whole thing got started. We started helping one family and then another and then another, and before long people heard about what we were doing and we started getting requests from families for help. Then I found out about some government housing projects in the South Beach area that were absolutely horrendous, and that there were a lot of Jewish families living there."

By this time the Shabbos Club—as it came to be known—was taking care of numerous families, and about sixty women were involved in preparing meals.

"When I returned to teaching it became hard for me to coordinate with all the women who were cooking food and bringing it over to our house. Instead, what I did was to contact various kosher food businesses to see if they could help. And that was great. Kosher hotels and restaurants and caterers and bakeries were all willing to donate food. And the stuff they donated was really nice."

"We would drive around collecting all this great food and then I'd load my kids into the car and we would drive to the housing projects. The poor Jewish people would come out and we'd give out all this food, and then from there we would make deliveries to other families."

"After a few years my Russian housekeeper suggested that we organize the food into individual boxes with the names of the families on their respective boxes. You see, people had begun to request certain kinds of food so we often needed to know what went to whom. My housekeeper offered to do the organization and labeling and that's how it works now. Each family gets their own box and we either deliver it or they pick it up."

Over the years numerous volunteers have enabled more than one hundred poor families to receive food, clothing and even furniture from the Shabbos Club. And of course Jewish holidays are a big time for the Shabbos Club. Before Purim people get *hamantaschen* and *mishloach manot* gift baskets, for Rosh Hashanah they get apples and honey, and for Passover they get enough Passover food to last the entire week.

"I'll tell you honestly, if I had known it was going to be like this I would have been totally petrified because I'm not such an organized person. But what happened was that you see a need and you feel like you want to help. It's very hard to sit down for a *yom tov* (holiday) meal if you know there are people who don't have food.

(Note: Today the official name of the Shabbos Club is Tomche Shabbos Fund Inc. Rachel Schwartz is a fictitious name.)

ROSE

If wrinkles told a person's age the way the rings of a tree do, then Rose would have to be about a hundred. And if a smile could bring out the sun, then wherever Rose went there would never be a cloud in the sky.

It takes Rose about twenty minutes to walk the half-block from her apartment to the bus stop on the corner—a little longer when it's raining and a lot longer when there is snow on the ground. But the walk doesn't bother Rose because she's got somewhere to go. Someone is waiting for her—for her touch and her smile.

Rose moves at about the same pace as a lot of the residents at Meadow Manor where she volunteers. When she arrives, the first person whose day is made brighter is the receptionist. And then Rose gets to work.

"I sit and talk and spend time with them. Even if they can't speak, I know it makes them feel good. Sometimes I'll help people to eat and there are some people who I always try to feed. I can just tell how good it makes them feel. There's one gentleman who just loves when I feed him pudding or ice cream."

In many ways it's not always easy for Rose to take care of herself these days, but it's even harder for her not to take care of others.

A CIRCUMCISION IN COLUMBUS

The very first *bris mila* (circumcision) in history was that of Abraham, the founder of the Jewish people. Abraham had his bris at the age of ninety-nine and it has always been considered a great act of *mesirat nefesh*, utter devotion. Ever since that first circumcision, Jews have displayed a deep devotion to the bris mila—the covenant of Abraham.

The members of the Rybashkin family are, for the most part, quiet and unassuming and have a particular quality that enables them to go almost unnoticed even in a small group of people. Their soft and gentle way belies an inner intensity that few people are aware of.

In Russia, Pavel Rybashkin and his son Daniel both had a bris mila, a circumcision when they were eight days old. In Russia, under the Communist regime, a Jewish ceremony such as a circumcision could have been considered a crime against the state. Allow your son to be circumcised and you could have lost your job, been barred from attending a university, been moved to an even smaller apartment than you already lived in or been thrown in jail. (After all, who knows what kind of state secrets were being passed to Zionist agents at those circumcisions?) But these threats did not stop the Rybashkins. When a son was born to the Rybashkin family they did what was necessary to arrange for a clandestine bris. Pavel Rybashkin's brother Motti did the same. When his sons Valery and Sam were born, he made sure to arrange for a bris for each of them too.

Most Jews in the Soviet Union were not like the Rybashkins. They were either too afraid of the authorities or knew too little about Judaism to take the step of having a circumcision.

A few years after receiving their visas to emigrate, the Rybashkins all settled in Columbus, Ohio. Not long after arriving in Columbus, Pavel's wife, Inna, gave birth to a beautiful baby boy.

Enter, Yaacov Chaikin.

Yaacov Chaikin's family came to the United States when

he was fifteen years old. His parents dutifully enrolled him in the local public school of their Columbus neighborhood and Yaacov was well on his way to becoming a full-fledged "new American." In Columbus, Yaacov's family joined a synagogue and Yaacov began to get interested in Judaism, the heritage he had never known. Yaacov was fortunate to meet a young dentist, Dr. Fox, (who also happened to be a rabbi) who was the director of the local NCSY (National Council of Synagogue Youth) chapter. Yaacov eventually became very involved in NCSY, and when he was eighteen he decided that he had to have a bris. Rabbi Fox arranged for Yaacov to go New York where a bris could be performed by a *mohel* named Rabbi Ashkenazi who is an expert at adult circumcision.

When Yaacov returned to Columbus he decided that he was going to devote himself, as best as he could, to the mitzvah of circumcision. To Yaacov this meant speaking to as many Russians as would listen about the beauty of being Jewish and the importance of having a circumcision. Now it's true that being a Jew is beautiful and circumcision is basic to Jewish identity, but still, a bris mila for a teenager is not an easy sell. Yet Yaacov was determined.

Over the next two years Yaacov spent hundreds of hours speaking to Russians about the importance of a bris mila. During that time over thirty Jews, ages seven to thirty-five, decided that if being a Jew meant having a circumcision then that was what they were going to to.

Now back to the Rybashkins.

Shortly after their son was born the Rybashkins asked Yaacov to help them arrange for their son's bris—the first public bris in the Rybashkin family in over fifty years. And Yaacov, being who he was, did far more than just call the local *mohel* and make the necessary arrangements. Yaacov spent the next week, day and night, organizing a community celebration.

Over two hundred people attended the bris of little Chaim Rybashkin. And what a powerful occasion it was. If you were an American Jew you couldn't help but ask yourself, Would I have taken the risk of giving my child a bris in the Soviet Union? And if you were a new American, you couldn't help but wonder, Maybe being a Jew is far more meaningful than I ever realized?

When the Rybashkin bris was over, Yaacov, who was exhausted from the whole week, stopped by the Schwartz house to unwind an get a bite to eat. A book on the shelf next to him caught his eye: <u>The Comprehensive Jewish Calendar</u>. This is a book of charts that synchronizes the Jewish calendar and the English calendar from the year 1900 to 2100. If, for example, you were born on August 3, 1961 and want to know what your Hebrew birthday is, you can look it up in <u>The Comprehensive Jewish Calendar</u>.

Yaacov opened the book and flipped the pages until he found his birthday, March 9, 1975. The corresponding Hebrew date is the twenty-sixth of Adar. At that point, Yaacov wondered out loud, "Let's see what the date of my bris was supposed to be. The date was the fourth of Nisan. And then Yaacov looked up the date of when his bris actually was. The English date was March 26, 1993—also the fourth of Nisan.

When Yaacov Chaikin was eight days old the Hebrew date was the fourth of Nisan, but he didn't have a bris. However, eighteen years later he felt compelled to have one. Though unbeknownst to him at the time, the bris that Yaacov chose to have took place on the very same date—eighteen years later—that his bris would have originally been scheduled for—the fourth of Nisan.

IT STARTED WITH PURIM

In 1962 Israel Katz moved to Israel. That same year, shortly before the holiday of Purim, he made a decision that would forever change his life and the lives of hundreds, if not thousands of people.

"The celebration of Purim includes a special mitzvah to give money to the poor, and I had recently met a man, let's call him Mr. Freund, who was in serious financial trouble. It was clear that he and his family needed some help. I decided that I would try to do something, and that Purim I asked everyone I met—in synagogue, on the street, on a bus—if they had some money that they could spare to help a needy family. And since it was Purim and there is this special mitzvah to help the poor, people were very generous."

A year later, unfortunately, the Freund family's situation had still not improved. Remembering what had taken place the year before, Mr. Katz decided that once again he would use Purim as an opportunity to raise money for a family in need. And once again, people were very generous and the Freunds had a brief respite from their financial burdens.

Another year passed and not long before Purim, Mr. Katz met Baruch Adelman. Baruch had recently lost his job and was faced with a large monthly rent to pay, all the other expenses of a young family and rapidly dwindling resources. That year, Mr. Katz decided, he would redouble his Purim fund raising efforts and do what he could to help both the Freund and the Adelman families. And this time he didn't stop with Purim. Before Passover arrived he decided to ask people he knew if they could help two families that were literally unable to take care of their basic food needs for Passover. And then, with Passover behind him and Rosh Hashanah fast approaching, once again Mr. Katz was quietly asking people if they could help two families who didn't have enough to provide for their families over the holidays.

By 1970 Israel Katz was providing one hundred and fifty needy families with the necessary funds to purchase food for Passover, Rosh Hashanah, Sukkot and of course, Purim.

Today Israel Katz, a full-time school teacher and father of twelve, works in his "spare time" to make sure that more than six hundred families a year have food for the holidays.

"I never imagined that I would be doing something like this but I'm sure it's God's will. It all started with one mitzvah on Purim and look what it led to."

"Unfortunately I don't have any big donors who give me lots of money so I have to spend many late nights on the phone calling people and asking for money. However, I no longer distribute the money personally. About fifteen years ago I created a coupon system with two grocery stores that give me a ten percent discount on everything in their stores. This way I just go to the store with a hundred thousand dollars and they give me a hundred and ten thousand dollars' worth of coupons that can be redeemed for anything in the store. I also have two wonderful friends who have volunteered their time to make sure that the coupons get delivered to the families. We deliver the coupons far enough in advance of the holidays so that the recipients are at least relieved of the anxiety of wondering how they will provide a nice Yom Tov (holiday) for their families."

"And I must tell you, one of the most gratifying things is that when people who we once helped get back on their feet, they often come to us—this time not for help, but rather to help someone else."

(For information on how to donate money to Mr. Katz, call Shimon Apisdorf at 410-653-7800)

CHANUKAH MARGARINE

At the conclusion of every sixteen-hour work day, in the hell called Bergen Belsen, the block commander liked to have some fun with his Jews.

The meal at the end of the day consisted of old dry bread, filthy watery soup and a pat of something like margarine made from vegetable fat. The margarine was scooped out of a large tub, and after the meal had been distributed and the tub was empty, the commander allowed the starving prisoners to jump into the empty tub and lick the remaining margarine from the walls of the tub. The sight of starving Jews licking up bits of margarine provided nightly entertainment for the commander and his guards.

One prisoner, however, refused to be a part of the commanders show. Though like all the rest he was a withered, starving shadow of a man aged far beyond his years, still, he would never allow himself to scavenge for a lick of margarine. The other prisoners called him Elijah. In some unspoken way, the others drew strength from Elijah's refusal to join the frenzy.

Then, one night, something happened that seemed to shatter whatever spirit remained in the prisoners. Elijah cracked. All at once he threw himself into the greasy vat and furiously rolled around like a crazed beast. And how the commander howled; it was a deep belly laugh of satanic satisfaction. The last of the Jews had been broken.

Later, after the guards had left and the Jews were in their barracks, Elijah pulled out a jacket and began to pluck off the buttons. The others looked on in silence—Elijah had gone mad. One by one he separated threads from the buttons of the jacket—and then he looked up.

His eyes were on fire. "Do you know what tonight is?"

he demanded. "Tonight is the first night of Chanukah and I've been saving little bits of fat to use as candles."

That night Elijah led the others in the lighting of the Chanukah flames. The candles were made of scraps of old margarine Elijah had saved; the wicks were made of thread; and the fresh margarine Elijah had furiously scavenged for that evening was the oil.

And Elijah's flames are still burning.

KISS ME

Yad B'Yad (Hand in Hand) is a volunteer organization that has been in existence for over twenty years. If you are sick at home and need someone to do the shopping for you, a Hand in Hand volunteer is there. If you are in the hospital, someone from Hand in Hand will be sure to visit you. You broke your leg and need a wheelchair, a Hand in Hand volunteer has a basement full of medical equipment that they lend out to anyone in need.

Mrs. Sarah Neuman has been coordinating the Hand in Hand volunteers and tells the following story about one of Hand in Hand's veteran volunteers, Leah Bacharach.

Mrs. Bacharach is in charge of organizing the weekly visits to patients in the hospital and of course she also goes to visit people herself. In addition to her hospital visits, Mrs. Bacharach also goes once a week to the Winding Way nursing hame to speak to people who have no family to visit them, help with feeding some of the weaker residents and do whatever she can to bring some smiles to anyone who hasn't yet smiled that week.

"When a lot of Russian immigrants started moving into our community, Mrs. Bacharach decided that she was going to teach herself some Russian so that she could make people feel comfortable when she met them. She bought a book that had simple Russian phrases in it and between that and picking up words here and there from the Russians, she began to build a vocabulary. One day, while looking through her Russian phrase book, she came across the words for 'kiss me.' Mrs. Bacharach didn't think she would ever have use for those words, so she went on to something else."

"A few weeks later, during one of her hospital visits, Mrs. Bacharach learned of an elderly Russian woman who was in the hospital. She approached one of the nurses and asked if she could go into the woman's room. The nurse told her that there wasn't any point because the woman was barely conscious, never opened her eyes and 'we're not even sure if she can hear anything.'

"Mrs. Bacharach told the nurse that she wanted to go in anyway. Inside the room she stood at the bedside of this very still and slowly breathing woman. She was standing there for a few minutes when the Russian words for kiss me, potselui meñay, came into her mind. She leaned over close to the woman's ear and said in Russian, 'kiss me.' Without opening her eyes, the old Russian woman puckered her lips to offer a kiss to her visitor."

Thanks to Mrs. Bacharach, the nurses were able to know for certain that the woman was still able to hear.

Donuts

Judy Waldman, a tenth grader at New York Hebrew Academy, registered for a special computer course that was offered two days a week after school. One day, on her way home from the course, Judy saw the owner of Danzigers Bakery throwing trays of donuts into a large garbage can on the sidewalk in front of his store. Judy had recently heard her parents speaking about the Bornstein family, a family that lived on the third floor of their building, that was having terrible financial difficulties. She asked the owner if she could have a bag of donuts for some children in a family that was going through tough times. He was happy to oblige.

Within a few weeks Judy and the owner of the bakery worked out an arrangement where she could come every day at 7:00, closing time, and pick out left over donuts that she would later deliver to Mrs. Bornstein. Mrs. Bornstein was reluctant to accept the charity but when Judy explained that it was all going to be wasted if she didn't take it, she agreed. And the Bornstein children were thrilled that they had a new after school snack of fresh donuts.

As it turned out, Judy's mother, Mrs. Freeda Waldman knew of a number of other families that were also in need. Soon, every day at 7:00, Freeda Waldman would be driving her daughter to the back of Danzigers Bakery where they would pick up bags of donuts, bagels and breads to distribute to the families who needed them.

Nora Cohen is one of the women whose family benefitted from the Waldman's kind efforts. These are her words:

"Today, thank God, my family no longer needs the assistance, so I help Freeda prepare some of the boxes for delivery. Freeda is the kind of person who has no time but somehow still manages to find time to help lots of people. Currently she is taking care of at least a dozen families, and not just with bread and donuts, with all their food needs."

Mr. Markowitz, the owner of a small grocery store down the block from Danzigers Bakery, found out about what was going on at the bakery and decided that he too wanted to be a part of the Waldman's efforts. He started by giving her some canned goods and extra produce. Eventually Mr.

Markovitz began intentionally over-ordering certain items from his suppliers, including chickens, so that he would always have plenty to give to the Waldman's.

"Once, when Freeda was going to be out of town, Mr. Markovitz offered to take over the deliveries for her but she refused. 'You must understand,' she explained, 'it's very painful for these families to accept help and I always tell them that they are really doing a mitzvah by not letting all this food go to waste. My children will handle all the deliveries while I'm away. The families all know them already and they won't be embarrassed if it's just them making the delivery.'

MIRACLES LARGE AND SMALL

God is not a supernal superhero with flowing white hair, a long beard and kind eyes who is waiting to swoop down and save every damsel in distress.

He is also not a show-off.

The Hebrew word for miracle is *nes*. The word *nes* literally means "banner." When a miracle happens it's as if someone is holding up a banner to catch your attention. Banners come in all sorts of shapes and sizes, and the same is true of miracles. When the Jewish people were trapped at the edge of the Red Sea with the Egyptian army bearing down on them, and then the sea split to let the Jews across, now that was a big banner. That wasn't just a driver at the airport holding a makeshift sign with an arriving passengers name on it; that was a state-of-the-art stadium scoreboard flashing all sorts of messages.

Compared to the splitting of the sea, the burning of one day's worth of oil for eight days wasn't such a big deal. But it was a banner nonetheless. Its purpose was to catch the attention of the Jewish people and to remind them of the presence of God in their lives.

As a rule, God is very subtle. Unless He absolutely has to, He doesn't go around splitting seas. Instead, like a small flame, He makes His presence felt in a quiet sort of way. Most people, at one time or another, have felt that in some way God was involved in their lives. They noticed a banner, a sign that flashed on for a moment and said, "Slow down for a moment. Think, feel and listen. Despite all appearances, there is far more to life than often meets the eye, and you can be a part of it."

The following stories were all related by the people who experienced them. I must warn you though, in none of these stories will you hear about a sea splitting or anything even remotely close. In each case the person felt the subtle presence of something beyond the normal workings of everyday life. In essence, each noticed a shell on the beach, picked it up, listened and heard the quiet sound of the ever-present sea. Perhaps you too remember such a moment. If you do, Chanukah is the perfect time to take that shell out of your drawer, listen again and remember what you heard. The tiny lights of Chanukah can serve to reconnect us to the tiny banners that dot our lives.

CHAVRUSA FOR ETERNITY

Two people who study Torah together all called *chavrusas*, study partners. The word *chavrusa* literally means "friend." This is the story of one man and his *chavrusa*.

Rabbi Eliezer Milstein came from a very poor family in Bilgorai, Poland. It was expected that after his bar mitzvah he would go right to work—but Eliezer had other ideas. Eliezer wanted to study the Torah, and at the age of thirteen he ran away to study in a *yeshiva* in Pinsk.

Travel was extremely difficult in Poland, and three years passed without Eliezer seeing his family. When World War II broke out, news reached Eliezer that the Germans had deported everyone in Bilgorai. Eliezer was overcome with guilt for not seeing his family and decided to return to Bilgorai. When he arrived, the Poles told him that his sister had been brutally murdered, that everyone else had been taken away and that he had better flee because the Germans would be back. Not knowing what else to do, Eliezer returned to Pinsk, but again he found nothing. The entire yeshiva had been deported. Everyone was gone.

Eliezer managed to find a group of students from another yeshiva, but soon they too, along with Eliezer, were arrested—this time by the Russians. The Russians considered any Jew with a Polish passport to be a spy, and as such their fate was slave labor in Siberia.

Yerachmiel, Eliezer's son, lives in New York.

"My father told us about how they were forced to dig ditches for which there was no need other than to make them work. On Shabbos my father also had to work or else he would have been killed, but he was determined to do something to preserve the Shabbos. In Jewish law if you do a forbidden activity in an unusual manner, though it's still not permissible, it's not as bad. My father decided that to honor the Shabbos he would hold his shovel in an awkward position. Unfortunately, a Russian guard saw him digging in this inefficient manner and began to beat him over the head with a truncheon. He survived the beating and was sent to work in the kitchen."

During the war there were widespread food shortages in Russia that led to massive starvation, but in Eliezer's case, this turned out to be a blessing in disguise. With little food available there wasn't much work in the kitchen and Eliezer and another Jewish prisoner, David Treibush, found themselves with time on their hands.

"My father always told us about how he had studied the Talmudic tractate (volume) of *Yuma*. He had managed to bring a tattered copy of Yuma with him to Siberia and whenever he and David Treibush had time they would study together."

The hell of World War II engulfed all of Europe, yet deep inside Siberia two chavrusas kept the light of Torah study glowing.

After the war these chavrusas lost touch, and even though they settled close to one another in New York, their relationship never resumed. Each went on to rebuild a new life and a new family in a new land.

Eliezer Milstein became a respected rabbi and educator, and later in life he purchased an apartment in Israel where he planned to retire.

"When my father passed away he left no instructions regarding his burial. He had recently purchased an apartment in Israel so we decided to have him buried in Jerusalem. We contacted my brother's wife's cousin in Jerusalem to help us arrange for a burial there. As it turned out he was able to find a plot on the Mount of Olives. This is the most revered Jewish cemetery in the world, and tens of thousands of people are buried there."

"One of my father's dearest friends, someone who had been with him in Siberia, came with me to Jerusalem for the burial. We made our way to the Mount of Olives, and as they were bringing my father close to his grave his old friend, who was walking next to me, began to faint. After I helped him recover he said, 'Who picked the grave?' 'What do you mean who picked the grave? 'It was one of my brother's cousins through marriage.' I said. 'Did he know your father? Did he know your father was in Siberia? Did he know about his life in Siberia?'

"I told him that this person knew nothing about my father."

"Look at the grave next to your father's. It's David Treibush, your father's chavrusa."

EXCUSE ME SANTA, IT'S TIME TO LIGHT THE MENORAH

Here's how Michael from California tells his story:

When I was living up in Santa Cruz County, I wanted to do a shabbos that was a little out of the ordinary, so I decided that I would take Shabbos with me down to Big Sur.

It was shabbos afternoon and I was on the beach meditating and watching the ocean. It was a very hot day. A woman and her two children came by. She asked me in a really humble, polite way if I had any juice to spare, not for herself but for the children. Of course I gave them what I had to drink. She was so grateful. She just kept saying, 'Thank you, thank you, may God bless you.' When she and the kids began to walk away she said good-bye, and I said, "Shalom."

Ordinarily I wouldn't say shalom to a stranger on the beach, but for some reason this time I did. When she heard me say shalom, she turned around and her eyes widened. It was like she was in shock. 'Shabbat shalom,' she said to me, and I said, 'Shabbat shalom.' The next thing you know we're sitting down and talking, and we ended up spending the whole day on the beach talking and talking and talking."

As it turned out Zariya (that was her name) and her children lived in a van. Zariya was Catholic, but she had been married to a Jewish man. She considered herself to be a spiritual person who believed in God. After she had children she decided that she would rather raise them as Jews, not as Catholics. There was one problem however. Zariya's husband wanted to have nothing to do with any sort of religion and forbade her from giving the children any type of Jewish education. This became a very contentious issue between them. Her husband also had a drinking problem and sometimes hit her and the children. Eventually she took the children and left.

Michael felt that he had to do something to help Zariya and her children. His roommate was going out of town for a few weeks, so he decided to invite them to stay with him for a while; maybe he could help her get back on her feet.

While Zariya and the children were staying with Michael, she insisted that Michael teach them something about Judaism. He did, and they loved it.

"Anyway, it was almost Chanukah, and the kids were already learning the blessings for the candles. Then one day she decided to take them out for lunch. They were late coming home and when she finally arrived, Zariya was hysterical, freaked out, and all she could say was, 'They took my children, they took my children.'

"After she calmed down a bit, she said that a private detective had taken the kids and she showed me his card. 'You don't understand,' she said. 'My husband has family out here in California that live in Sacramento. They're very rich and probably decided to hire a detective to track me down and take the kids.'

"And that's exactly what had happened. Zariya called her husband's parents, and her husband was there with the kids. He wouldn't let her speak with them. He called her a dangerous religious fanatic and threatened to report her to the police. She was crushed.

"So a day passes and she decides to call again, and she

wants me to get on the line because the husband is very suspicious about who I am. I was able to convince him I was a very normal, decent person, and we negotiated to come up to Sacramento to see the kids one time for Chanukah. We promised to stay for just fifteen minutes, light the menorah with the kids, and then leave."

On the way up to Sacramento, Zariya told Michael about her in-laws.

"They are good people and she respects them, even if they do celebrate Christmas every year. "If my husband wants the kids," she said, "that's fine. I'll agree to that as long as they're living with their grandparents because they're decent people. The only thing I'm worried about is that they're going to grow up celebrating Christmas and hearing from their father about what a terrible person their mother is—how she's poor and has nothing to offer them. All I want is for them to have a little godliness."

When Michael and Zariya pulled up the driveway they were very nervous. They had wanted to bring some nice presents but didn't have enough money for what they wanted. Instead, all they brought with them was a small disposable menorah and some candles.

"So we pull up to the home and she says, 'I'm just warning you;you won't even believe this is a Jewish family.' 'It's okay,' I tell her, and we walk to the front door and ring the bell. We can hear the kids running to the door. The kids open the door and give us these big hugs, and while they're hugging us, the grandparents and the father were just eyeballing us in a very cold way. After a moment I look around and I'm just blown away because I'm looking right into a whole living room full of toys. There was a pile of presents with Christmas wrapping, and an enormous tree, and the grandfather is dressed in a Santa Clause outfit.

"Now we only had fifteen minutes to spend there and I

really wanted to make an impact on these kids, so we went right over to the bar to set up the menorah. I taught them everything I could in the little time we had, and they were just all smiles and listening to everything I said. I showed them exactly how to set up the candles, and before we began to light I asked the grandmother to turn off the lights. So there we are, lighting the candles and making the blessings and trying to sing ma'otzur together with the kids.

"When we were done the kids wanted more so I told them that there was a special mitzvah to just look at the candles and enjoy the light because it's God's light. So there we were just standing and gazing at those candles. When I looked over at the kid's father, I saw that he wouldn't look either of us in the eye; he just looked down at the ground. And the grandparents are holding hands; she's got tears in her eyes, and he has taken off his Santa Claus hat and beard."

An uneasy silence filled the room, and then it was time for Zariya and Michael to leave. On the way out, Zariya's husband said that he wanted to talk to her for a minute.

"Zariya," he said in a soft voice, "I felt something when we were looking at those candles. I promise that tomorrow I'm going to find a Hebrew school for the kids, and I'll make sure they get an education"

POSTSCRIPT: Zariya went on to study more about Judaism and eventually decided to convert. Before going through with the conversion she needed to speak with her grandmother who was a strict Catholic and with whom she was very close; her mother had died years earlier in an accident and she never knew her father. Zariya called her grandmother and was apologizing and trying to explain at the same time when her grandmother began to cry.

"Zariya," she began through her tears, "I've never told

you this and I swore I never would, but now I must. When I was a young woman I had just been married when the war broke out. They put us in the camps and my husband and my entire family were wiped out. I swore to myself that if I ever married again I would never allow my family to suffer the same fate. After the war I met this wonderful man. He wasn't Jewish, but he took care of me and we got married. I told him I could never raise my children as Jews. Your mother never knew she was Jewish. Zariya, you don't have to convert. You already are a Jew."

FOOD FOR SHABBOS

Mr. Albert Azar of Deal Park, New Jersey, was working as a salesman for a children's wear company. Business took Mr. Azar all over the country and there were times when this posed a challenge because of the fact that he kept kosher. In most major cities there wasn't much of a problem finding kosher food, it was his trips to the south that were particularly challenging.

"Whenever I had to travel down south on business I always arranged to spend Shabbos in Memphis. There was a kosher restaurant in Memphis and before Shabbos I would order enough food to last me for the following week of traveling."

Once, in 1972, Mr. Azar had to begin one of his trips with a stop in Birmingham, Alabama. His plan was to go to Memphis after Birmingham and then, after Shabbos, to finish the rest of his trip. In Birmingham, after meeting with all his usual customers, he decided to try and get an appointment with the president of a large corporation who on all his previous trips had never agreed to meet with him.

"Azar," the president of the corporation said, "I need to

speak with you, I've been getting a lot of calls about your line of merchandise."

Albert Azar was in luck and soon had an appointment scheduled for one o'clock that afternoon. It was a Thursday.

Unfortunately for Mr. Azar, the president had some other meetings that ran longer than expected. After a few hours the president came out of his office to apologize and asked if they could reschedule their meeting for the next morning.

"Tomorrow is Friday and it's very important that I catch an early plane for Memphis," Mr. Azar said.

"No problem, we can meet first thing in the morning."

The next morning Mr. Azar arrived at nine o'clock sharp and once again he was kept waiting. As the hours wore on he became concerned about making it to Memphis for shabbos and about having food for the next week of his trip. Mr. Azar decided to call the kosher restaurant in Memphis to place his order, but to his great consternation he was told that the restaurant had just closed and there was no way he could get any food until Sunday. He walked into the president's office. "I'm taking the next flight to Memphis, if you want to place an order do it now because I'm leaving." The president gave him a small order and returned to his phone conversation.

In Memphis Mr. Azar had reservations at an inexpensive hotel where he always stayed. When he pulled up to the hotel he made a quick decision to stay at the new hotel across the street. "I don't have any food for shabbos." he thought to himself "so I may as well have a nice place to stay."

"Do you have any rooms available?" he asked the woman at reception.

"We're practically empty," she said, "you can have any room you want."

"Look" said Mr. Azar, "I'm really running late, just give

me any room please."

In a minute he was on his way to room 358. There was hardly any time before sunset, when shabbos begins, and Mr. Azar threw his bags on the bed and went to hang a few things in the closet. And that is when he thought that he must have begun hallucinating. "The pressure of the last twenty-four hours must have gotten to me," he thought. Mr. Azar closed the closet door, waited a moment and then slowly opened it again. There, on the shelf in the closet, was a bottle of kosher wine, two challahs (loaves of shabbos bread), six types of deli meats, potato salad, soda, cole slaw, and cookies. Plenty of food for shabbos and then some.

Three months later: Mr. Azar was at a get-together at his friend Abe Kassin's house. During the course of the evening he overheard Jack Harrari say, "By the way Abe, did you ever find out what happened to all that food you left in the hotel in Memphis?" Mr. Azar spun around and asked Abe what they were talking about.

Abe explained. "A few months ago, Ike Hillery and I were in Memphis on business. Before shabbos we bought enough food to last us for the following week. Early that afternoon I came down with unbearable stomach pains and, not wanting to go to a strange hospital in Memphis, I caught a plane back to New Jersey. Ike arranged everything for us but in all the hurry we forgot about the food we had bought."

"I can tell you what happened to your food." said Mr. Azar.

"What do you mean?" asked Abe.

"I ate it!"[11]

BILLY JOEL, A CHANGE IN AIRLINES AND A REFUSENIK

Before the collapse of the Soviet Union it was illegal for Jews there to study or practice Judaism or to emigrate to Israel. Those who dared to apply for an exit visa knew that they risked their jobs, their safety and their future. Most were routinely refused permission to leave. These people became known as Refuseniks.

One of the few ways that a Jew could leave the Soviet Union was for the sake of family reunification. Soviet Jews who had immediate family abroad were sometimes allowed to join them.

Stuart Wax works in the music industry in Los Angeles. In 1987 he heard about a Jewish woman in the Soviet Union who wanted to leave. Stuart decided that he was going to travel to the Soviet Union to marry this woman, and then after returning to the states he would request that his wife be allowed to join him.

"I had this mission, but I had no idea when I was going or how the whole thing would happen. At the time I was working with Rabbi Abraham Cooper of the Simon Weisenthal Center in Los Angeles. We were trying to organize a concert with big name performers for the cause of Soviet Jewry. I started looking for articles that had anything to do with music and the Soviet Union. One day I came across an article in Billboard magazine about Billy Joel taking his "Bridge" concert tour to Russia. I taped the article to my wall. Not long after cutting out that article I woke up one morning thinking, "That's my ticket. Billy Joel is going to Russia in July because that's when I'm supposed to go."

Stuart called Billy Joel's manager and claimed to be a journalist writing for college newspapers around the country. He told the manager that he thought Billy Joel's tour was a historic event and that he wanted to get a visa and travel with the band and cover the tour.

"He said he was very sorry, that it was too late and the visas were already issued. There was nothing he could do to help. I heard that to get a Soviet visa you needed a voucher from a Moscow hotel. A friend of mine who is a travel agent helped me out with that, so I flew up to San Francisco where the Soviet embassy was. I told them that I was with the Billy Joel tour and showed them the hotel vouchers. Unfortunately, what I needed was a voucher from the Soviet Intourist agency, not just from any travel agent. They threw me out.

"My next step didn't make a lot of sense, but I tried it anyway. Ronnie Vance had recently been hired as president of Geffen Music Publishing, and I had met him through some friends in the Jewish community a few months earlier. Neither Ronnie or Geffen Records had anything to do with Billy Joel, but I went to speak with him anyway. I told Ronnie that I was going to Russia to marry this Refusenik and that I needed a letter from him saying, "Stuart Wax is a guest of the Billy Joel tour. Please afford him all the necessary visas and documents." Ronnie said he didn't know why he was writing the letter, that it made no sense but that he wanted to be a part of the mitzvah."

With that letter Stuart was able to obtain his prized visa. A short time later, with his luggage packed with illegal items like prayer books and *tefillin*, Stuart and his friend Jerry Katz were on their way to Frankfurt where they would connect with a direct flight to Moscow.

"When we arrived in Frankfurt the Lufthansa people told us that all flights to Moscow had already departed and that we would have to wait there until the next morning. I told Jerry that there was a reason for this, we just don't know what it is.

"The next morning we went to Lufthansa and there were a bunch of Americans hanging out. They asked us why we were going to Russia. We weren't going to say we were going to do a mitzvah, so we said that we were journalists going to cover the Billy Joel tour. "That's funny," they said, "we're Mark Rivera and Liberty DeVitto." Mark was Billy's horn player and Liberty was his drummer. There were some other people from the tour with them too.

"It's weird," they said to me, "We weren't even supposed to be here. We were all in London waiting to fly Aeroflot directly to Moscow, and all of a sudden they said that some of us would have to fly Lufthansa through Frankfurt."

"When we arrived in Moscow and it came time to check our luggage through customs I got really nervous. I had all this illegal stuff with me, and I knew if I got caught I might never make it into the country. I was standing in line at passport control and from another line I heard one of the Billy Joel people yell, "Hey, King Cohen is here, King Cohen is here." It turned out that King Cohen—his name was really Steve Cohen—was Billy's road manager and was waiting to help clear everyone through customs.

"I walked over to this Steve Cohen guy and I said, "Steve, can you help us?" He said, "What's your name?" I said, "Stuart Wax" He said, "Give me your passport and your tickets and put your stuff with ours."

"The woman from customs came back and said there was a problem. All of the visas said "guest of the government," but ours only said "tourist." Steve Cohen said, "That's okay, they're with us. Their visas just came in late." So she let us go through and never even checked our luggage. After we all cleared customs, Billy Joel's publicist came over to us and said, "I don't know who you guys are, but you're on your own now."

During his stay in the Soviet Union, Stuart met with a number of Refuseniks, delivered his Jewish contraband and also got engaged. Three months later he returned to the Soviet Union to be married, and five months after their marriage Stuart's wife was able to join him in America, where they remained married until she was able to obtain political asylum.

A number of other things also happened while Stuart was in the Soviet Union. This is one of them:

"One night during our stay in Moscow, Jerry and I decided to go to a hotel and have a drink at a bar. While we were there we overheard two Americans talking about the Grateful Dead, which happens to be my all-time favorite band. We went over and started talking to these guys, and it turns out that they were Billy Joel's accountant and another guy from the tour. Then, all of the sudden the whole band, including Billy came over and sat down at our table. In the course of the conversation Billy says, "We've got to meet some real people.""

"The next day Jerry and I arranged for some of the band members to meet with some Soviet Jews in a Moscow park. One of the Jews was a Refusenik and a piano player who had his hand beaten."

Billy's guitarist, Russell Gavers, was very moved by the meeting. A year later on the night that Billy Joel's Moscow concert aired on HBO, Russell Gavers held a press conference together with the Student Struggle for Soviet Jewry to protest the treatment of Soviet Jews.

"I had started out trying to arrange a concert to create awareness about the plight of Soviet Jews. Then I got this idea to marry a Refusenik so she could escape the Soviet Union; and somehow, thank God, it all came to be."

SPLITTING THE RED SEA

Growing up in Poland, Herman Rosenblat witnessed pogroms, had to fight his way through school, and was accused by local priests of being a Christ killer. In 1939 he was imprisoned by the Germans, and in 1944 he was transferred to the Schlieben concentration camp seventy miles south of Berlin.

Roma's situation was much different. Her family was one of the few Jewish families who were helped by a priest, and they were all living as Christians and working on a farm that bordered Schlieben.

One day Herman spotted Roma, who was eight years old at the time, walking near the fence that separated the camp from the farmers' fields. In German, he asked her if she could bring him some food, but she didn't understand German. He then tried Polish, and this time she understood.

The next day they met again at the same place, and this time Roma brought an apple, a piece of bread and some water. Their encounter was a dangerous one, particularly for Herman. They had no time to talk, but Roma said she would be back again the next day.

Their brief meetings went on for seven months, and all the time Herman thought he was being helped by a kind Christian girl. One day Herman told Roma that he was being transferred to the Therensienstadt concentration camp in Czechoslovakia and that she shouldn't come back anymore. Roma, knowing that she would never see him again, began to cry. Herman, fearful that he might soon starve to death, also began to cry.

In 1945, after being liberated by the Russians, Herman went to England and from there made his way to Palestine. Roma and her family had also gone to Palestine. The war for

Israel's independence broke out in 1948. Herman fought as a soldier in the war, and Roma served as a nurse. They met and went out twice together with a group of friends without ever realizing who the other was.

"I was fighting in the army and I didn't know if I was going to be around, so I really didn't care to get involved with anyone," said Herman.

In July of 1957, now living in New York City, Roma was set up by a friend on a blind date. The date was with Herman Rosenblat, though again neither recognized one another.

Herman recalled, "It was love at first sight." As their conversation progressed they realized that they had both been in Germany during the war, he in a concentration camp and she on a farm pretending to be a Christian. Roma told about how she had brought food to a prisoner at the fence of the camp.

"What did he look like?" Herman wanted to know, "What did you bring him to eat?" Finally Herman asked her, "Did he tell you that he was being transferred to Therensienstadt and not to come back anymore?"

Suddenly it all became clear.

That very night Herman asked Roma to marry him. They have been married for thirty-eight years and have two children and one adorable grandson.[12]

> *Rabbi Yosi bar Halafta said: For God to bring together a suitable couple is as difficult as splitting the Red Sea.*
>
> Midrash

HOW DID YOU KNOW?

This is a story about *mesirat nefesh*, selfless dedication to a higher goal, and a small miracle.

There is an organization in Baltimore, Maryland known as Ahavas Yisroel—Jewish brotherly love. Ahavas Yisroel raises and distributes over $300,000.00 a year to families in need. It provides food packages for families who have fallen on hard times, pays utility bills, makes mortgage payments to help people keep their homes and provides job training and placement. Of the $300,000.00 dollars that Ahavas Yisroel raises annually, not one dollar is paid to it's staff. That's because there is no staff. Ahavas Yisroel is staffed solely by volunteers who are devoted to discretely helping families in need.

Eli Schlossberg, a member of the Ahavas Yisroel executive committee, related the following story about two families.

Family one: The Hartstein family was going through a real tough time. Dave Hartstein had been with the Allied Wire Co. for thirty years when the company went out of business, and it was very difficult for him to find a position that payed even close to what he was used to making. The Hartstein's however, just couldn't bring themselves to ask for help. They had lived in the community for years, their children grew up there and they just couldn't put out their hands and ask for charity.

"Often times," explained Mr. Schlossberg, "instead of delivering the money ourselves, we ask one of the rabbis in the community to do it. That way the family doesn't know who it's coming from and it takes away a lot of the embarrassment."

A check for the Hartstein family was delivered to the rabbi of the synagogue where the Hartsteins were members.

Family two: Saul Hartstein was injured in a car accident and was unable to work for many months. As the sole proprietor of a small business, Saul Hartstein soon found dwindling income and mounting bills. An Ahavas Yisroel volunteer learned that the family was under a lot of pressure and suggested that the organization offer some help.

The rabbi took the check from the Ahavas Yisroel volunteer, looked up Saul Hartstein's address in the synagogue directory, and drove over to the house. The rabbi held an envelope in his hand and rang the doorbell. When Dave Hartstein opened the door the rabbi immediately realized that in his haste he had looked at the address for the wrong Hartstein family.

Dave Hartstein was very moved to see his rabbi there on his doorstep holding an envelope. Before the rabbi could say anything, Dave Hartstein said in a quiet voice, "How did you know rabbi, how did you know we needed the help?"

A GREAT MIRACLE HAPPENED HERE

December 25, 1938 was a day for celebration around the world. For most of the people who celebrated it was Christmas, for a much smaller number of people it was Chanukah and for the Geier family it was the day they would escape the murderous clutches of the Germans. Shortly after Kristallnacht the Geier's received their passport and visa to leave Germany for the United States.

It was a sunny but cold day as their train bound for Holland pulled out of the Berlin station. The Geier's shared their second class compartment with two very stern looking Germans. Arnold Geier, age twelve and his sister, aged fifteen sat quietly with their parents. In a whisper, Arnold overheard his mother reassure his father that God would forgive him for not lighting his menorah that night. Mr. Geier was a cantor and a devout Jew and had packed a small menorah and some candles in his briefcase.

"Not long after darkness," recalls Arnold, "the train

slowed and puffed it's way into a special railway station at the German-Dutch border. We braced ourselves for our final encounter with the German police, Nazis and Gestapo. Just a few more miles and our old lives would be behind us."

The train sat in the station and the Geier's watched as the Border Police and the Gestapo carefully compared lists and prepared to check everyone's passports and papers.

"Finally, small groups of officers boarded the train for their inspection. Papa looked tense and broke out in a sweat. I was afraid. Suddenly, without any warning, all the lights in the station and on the train went out. A number of people lit matches for light and the glow on their faces was an eerie sight. Within moments the lights would flicker out and their faces were dark again. I felt like screaming."

In the confusion Mr. Geier stood up, managed to find his overcoat and pulled eight small candles out of his coat pocket. He struck a match and lit one candle. Using that candle he warmed the bottoms of the other candles and lined up all eight candles on the window sill of our compartment. He quietly recited the Chanukah blessings, lit the candles and then placed the eighth one off to the side of the others.

"For the first time in a long time, I saw a smile appear on Papa's face. Then someone shouted,'There's light over there!' The Border Police and the Gestapo men soon came to our compartment and used the light of the candles to conduct their checking of the passports and papers. One of the officers commended Papa on his resourcefulness for thinking ahead and packing 'travel candles.'

"About a half hour passed and then, as suddenly as they had gone off, the lights flickered on again. The officers thanked Papa and left our compartment to finish their work throughout the train."

"Remember this moment," Papa said to me, "like in the time of the Maccabees, a great miracle happened here."[12]

LET'S LIGHT: A STEP-BY-STEP GUIDE TO LIGHTING THE MENORAH

HOW TO ARRANGE YOUR CANDLES

On the first night one candle is placed at the far right side of the menorah. On all subsequent nights a new candle is added to the left of the last candle lit on the previous night. When lighting the candles the newest candle is lit first, then progressing to your right, the rest of the candles are lit. (In a nutshell: Add candles from right to left and light them from left to right.)

THE BLESSINGS

On the first night, the *shamesh* is lit and three blessings are said before lighting the menorah. On all subsequent nights only two blessings are said. The third blessing, *she'hechiyanu*, is omitted after the first night. (The *she'hechiyanu* blessing is a statement of joy and gratitude that we are again able to

celebrate Chanukah and is said only when we first usher in the
new holiday with the first night's lighting.)

BLESSING #1.

The Mitzvah of Kindling the Menorah.
This is said every night prior to lighting the menorah.

בָּרוּךְ אַתָּה יהוה אֱלֹהֵינוּ מֶלֶךְ הָעוֹלָם, אֲשֶׁר קִדְּשָׁנוּ
בְּמִצְוֹתָיו,וְצִוָּנוּ לְהַדְלִיק נֵר שֶׁל חֲנֻכָּה.

**Blessed are You, Adonai our God, King of the Universe, Who has
made us holy through His commandments, and has commanded us
to kindle the light of Chanukah.**

*Baruch atah Adonai, eloheynu melech ha-olam, asher kidshanu
b'mitzvotav, v'tzivanu l'hadlik ner shel Chanukah.*

BLESSING #2.

The Blessing for the Miracle.
This is said every night immediately after the first blessing
and before lighting the menorah.

בָּרוּךְ אַתָּה יהוה אֱלֹהֵינוּ מֶלֶךְ הָעוֹלָם, שֶׁעָשָׂה נִסִים לַאֲבוֹתֵינוּ,
בַּיָּמִים הָהֵם בַּזְּמַן הַזֶּה.

**Blessed are You, Adonai our God, King of the Universe, Who did
miracles for our forefathers, in those days at this very time.**

*Baruch atah Adonai, eloheynu melech ha-olam, sheh-asa nisim
la'avotaynu, ba'yamim ha-haim ba'zman ha-zeh.*

BLESSING #3.

The Blessing of Gratitude.
This blessing is said only on the first night . It is
recited after the second blessing, before the menorah is lit.

בָּרוּךְ אַתָּה יהוה אֱלֹהֵינוּ מֶלֶךְ הָעוֹלָם, שֶׁהֶחֱיָנוּ וְקִיְּמָנוּ וְהִגִּיעָנוּ
לַזְּמַן הַזֶּה.

Blessed are You, Adonai our God, King of the Universe, Who has kept us alive, sustained us and enabled us to arrive at this season.

Baruch atah Adonai, eloheynu melech ha-olam, sheh-heh-cheyanu, v'kiy'manu, v'higianu la'zman ha-zeh.

HA'NAYROT HA'LALU: THESE LIGHTS

The following song is read or sung after the menorah is lit. In some homes the song is begun after the first candle is lit and the singing continues while the remaining candles are being kindled; in other homes the singing begins only after all the candles have been lit. Either way is fine.

הַנֵּרוֹת הַלָּלוּ אֲנַחְנוּ מַדְלִיקִין עַל הַנִּסִים וְעַל הַנִּפְלָאוֹת,
וְעַל הַתְּשׁוּעוֹת וְעַל הַמִּלְחָמוֹת, שֶׁעָשִׂיתָ לַאֲבוֹתֵינוּ בַּיָּמִים הָהֵם
בַּזְּמַן הַזֶּה, עַל יְדֵי כֹּהֲנֶיךָ הַקְּדוֹשִׁים. וְכָל שְׁמוֹנַת יְמֵי חֲנֻכָּה, הַנֵּרוֹת
הַלָּלוּ קֹדֶשׁ הֵם. וְאֵין לָנוּ רְשׁוּת לְהִשְׁתַּמֵּשׁ בָּהֶם, אֶלָּא לִרְאוֹתָם
בִּלְבָד, כְּדֵי לְהוֹדוֹת וּלְהַלֵּל לְשִׁמְךָ הַגָּדוֹל עַל נִסֶּיךָ וְעַל נִפְלְאוֹתֶיךָ
וְעַל יְשׁוּעָתֶךָ.

HA'NAYROT HA'LALU *a'nu madlikin al ha'nisim v'al-ha'niflaot, v'al-ha'tshuot v'al-ha'milchamot, she'asiyta la-avoteinu ba-yamim ha-haim ba-zman ha-zeh, al y'day kohanecha ha-k'doshim. V'kol shmonas y'may chanukah ha-nayrot ha-lalu kodesh haim, v'ayn lanu reshut l'hishtamesh ba-hem ayla lirotam bilvad, k'day l'hodot u'l'hallel l'shimcha ha-gadol al neisecha v'al nif'lotecha v'al yishu-atecha.*

These lights *we kindle because of the miracles, the wonders, the salvations and the battles that You performed for our forefathers in those days, at this very time, through your holy Kohanim. For all eight days of Chanukah—these lights—they are holy; and we are not permitted to use them: Rather, only to look at them, in order to express gratitude and praise to Your great name; for Your miracles, Your wonders and Your salvations.*

MA'OTSUR: O' MIGHTY STRONGHOLD

After the menorah has been lit, the following song is read or sung out loud.

This song is divided into six stanzas. The first stanza is a prayer for the re-establishment of the Temple in Jerusalem as the center of Jewish spirituality. The next four stanzas are about various exiles experienced by the Jewish people, and the final stanza is a plea for the final redemption of the Jewish people.

מָעוֹז צוּר יְשׁוּעָתִי
תִּכּוֹן בֵּית תְּפִלָתִי
לְעֵת תָּכִין מַטְבֵּחַ
אָז אֶגְמוֹר בְּשִׁיר מִזְמוֹר

לְךָ נָאֶה לְשַׁבֵּחַ,
וְשָׁם תּוֹדָה נְזַבֵּחַ,
מִצָּר הַמְנַבֵּחַ,
חֲנֻכַּת הַמִּזְבֵּחַ.

רְעוֹת שָׂבְעָה נַפְשִׁי בְּיָגוֹן כֹּחִי כִּלָּה,
חַיַּי מֵרְרוּ בְקֹשִׁי בְּשִׁעְבּוּד מַלְכוּת עֶגְלָה,
וּבְיָדוֹ הַגְּדוֹלָה הוֹצִיא אֶת הַסְּגֻלָּה
חֵיל פַּרְעֹה וְכָל זַרְעוֹ יָרְדוּ כְּאֶבֶן בִּמְצוּלָה.

דְּבִיר קָדְשׁוֹ הֱבִיאַנִי וְגַם שָׁם לֹא שָׁקַטְתִּי,
וּבָא נוֹגֵשׂ וְהִגְלַנִי כִּי זָרִים עָבַדְתִּי,
וְיַיִן רַעַל מָסַכְתִּי כִּמְעַט שֶׁעָבַרְתִּי,
קֵץ בָּבֶל, זְרֻבָּבֶל, לְקֵץ שִׁבְעִים נוֹשַׁעְתִּי.

כְּרוֹת קוֹמַת בְּרוֹשׁ בִּקֵּשׁ אֲגָגִי בֶּן הַמְּדָתָא,
וְנִהְיָתָה לוֹ לְפַח וּלְמוֹקֵשׁ וְגַאֲוָתוֹ נִשְׁבָּתָה,
רֹאשׁ יְמִינִי נִשֵּׂאתָ וְאוֹיֵב שְׁמוֹ מָחִיתָ,
רֹב בָּנָיו וְקִנְיָנָיו עַל הָעֵץ תָּלִיתָ.

יְוָנִים נִקְבְּצוּ עָלַי אֲזַי בִּימֵי חַשְׁמַנִּים,
וּפָרְצוּ חוֹמוֹת מִגְדָּלַי וְטִמְּאוּ כָּל הַשְּׁמָנִים,
וּמִנּוֹתַר קַנְקַנִּים נַעֲשָׂה נֵס לַשּׁוֹשַׁנִּים,
בְּנֵי בִינָה יְמֵי שְׁמוֹנָה קָבְעוּ שִׁיר וּרְנָנִים.

חֲשׂוֹף זְרוֹעַ קָדְשֶׁךָ וְקָרֵב קֵץ הַיְשׁוּעָה,
נְקֹם נִקְמַת דַּם עֲבָדֶיךָ מֵאֻמָּה הָרְשָׁעָה,
כִּי אָרְכָה לָנוּ הַיְשׁוּעָה וְאֵין קֵץ לִימֵי הָרָעָה,
דְּחֵה אַדְמוֹן בְּצֵל צַלְמוֹן הָקֵם לָנוּ רוֹעִים שִׁבְעָה.

Ma'otsur *y'shu-ati le-cha na-eyh l'shabeach*
Tikon bays t'filati v'sham todah n'zabeach
L'ait ta-chiyn mat'bayach mi-tsar hamna-bayach
Az eg-mor b'shir miz'mor chanukat ha-mizbayach

Rah'os *savah nafshi b'yagon kochi kilah*
Cha'yay mai'r'rue b'koshi b'shiybud malchut eglah
U'vyado ha-gedolah hotsi et ha-segulah
Chayl paroh v'chol za'ro yar'du k'evayn biym'tsulah

D'vir *kad shoh he-vi'yani v'gam sham lo sha-ka't'ti*
U'va nogaysh v'higlani ki zariym ah-vah'd'dti
V'yayn ra-al ma-sachti ki-mat she-avarti
Kaitz ba-vel zeru-ba-vel l'kaytz shivim no-sha'ti

K'ros *ko'mas b'rosh bi'kaysh ah-gahgi bayn ha-midasah*
V'nisah lo l'fach u'l'mokesh v'ga-vato nishbata
Rosh y'mini ni'sayta v'oyaiv sh'mo ma-chiyta
Rov banav v'kinyanav al ha-eitz ta-liyta

Y'vanim *nik-b'itzu ah-lai ah-zai bi'may chash'manim*
U'fartzu chomot mig'dalai v'timu kol ha-shmanim
U'mi-notar kan-kanim naseh nes l'sho-shanim
Bi'may bina y'may shmona kavu shir u'r'nanim

Cha-sof *zroa kad'shecha v'karaiv kaitz ha-yeshua*
Nikom nik'mat dam av'decha may'uma ha-risha-ah
Ki archa lanu ha-yeshua v'aiyn kaitz l'may ha-ra-ah
D'chay ad'mon b'tsail tsalmon ha-kaym lanu roiym shivah

I. Prayer for the Re-establishment of the Temple
O' mighty stronghold who is my salvation,
    it is a delight to praise You.
Restore the house of my prayer,
    and there we will bring an offering of gratitude.
In the time that you will prepare the slaughter
    of the blaspheming oppressor;
Then I will complete a melodious song
    for the dedication of the altar.

II. The Bondage of Egypt
My soul was filled with hardships,
    my strength was sapped in grief.
They embittered my life with abuse,
    in the bondage of the kingdom that
      venerated the calf.
But through His great hand
    He brought out the precious ones,
The army of Pharaoh and his offspring
    sunk like a stone in the deep.

III. The Babylonian Exile
He brought me to the holy Temple (in Jerusalem),
    Yet even there I had no tranquility.
For an oppressor came and exiled me,
    all because I served alien gods;
And indulged in wine.
Shortly after my departure,
Babylon came to an end and Zerubavel (my leader) came.
At the end of seventy years I was saved.

IV. Persia and the Purim Miracle
To cut the towering cypress (Mordechai),
    this was the desire of the Aggagite (Haman) the son
    of Hamedasa.
But his plot trapped and ensnared him,
    and his arrogance was halted.

The leader of Benjamin You lifted,
    as for the enemy; his name was obliterated.
His many children and his property:
    You hung them on the gallows.

V. The Miraculous Chanukah Victory

The Greeks gathered against me,
    then, in the days of the Hasmoneans.
They breached the walls of my tower,
    and defiled all of the oil.
And from the one remaining flask
    a miracle occurred for the Jews.
The great sages of insight: Eight days,
    they established for song and celebration.

VI. Plea for the Final Redemption

Display Your Divine power,
    and hasten the culmination; the salvation.
Avenge the blood of Your servants from the evil nation.
For salvation has been long delayed,
    and the evil days are seem endless,
Repel the red one—our oppressor—into the shadows;
    renew and re-establish our leaders.

Notes

1) *The Founders of the Western World:* A History of Greece and Rome*: Intro.* Michael Grant, Scribners, 1991.
2) *The Oxford History of Greece and the Hellenistic World: 360.* John Boardman, Jasper Griffin, Oswyn Murray, Oxford University Press, 1991.
3) *History of the Second World War*: Winston Churchill,Houghton Mifflin, 1951.
4) *The Founders of the Western World:* A History of Greece and Rome: *16.* Michael Grant, Scribners, 1991.
5) *From Socrates to Sartre:* The Philosophic Quest: *54.* T.Z. Levine, Bantam, 1984.
6) *The Life of Greece: 669.* Will Durant, Simon and Schuster, 1939.
7) *The Oxford History of Greece and the Hellenistic World: 372.* John Boardman, Jasper Griffin, Oswyn Murray, Oxford University Press, 1991.
8) *The Oxford History of Greece and the Hellenistic World: 398.* John Boardman, Jasper Griffin, Oswyn Murray, Oxford University Press, 1991.
9) *The Pledge:* Leonard Slater, Simon and Schuster, 1970.
10) *Circumcision* from *Hassidic Tales of the Holocaust,* Yaffa Eliach, Avon Books, 1982.
11) Based on, *Food from Heaven* from *Visions of Greatness,* Yosef Weiss, CIS, 1993. Permission by Mr. Albert Azar.
12) Based on, *A Miraculous Love Story,* from *Beshert Magazine,* Leslie Russell, 1996.
13) *From Darkness to Light,* from *Heroes of the Holocaust,* Arnold Geier, London Books, 1993.

CHANUKAH REFLECTIONS

THE SURVIVAL KIT FAMILY HAGGADAH
by Shimon Apisdorf
The only Haggadah in the world…
Featuring the Matzahbrei Family. A loveable family of matzah people that guide you and your family through a delightful, insightful, spiritual and fun seder. **Featuring** the "talking Haggadah." A revolutionary translation. Never again will you read a paragraph in the Haggadah and say, "Huh, what's that supposed to mean?"
Written as a companion to the *Passover Survival Kit*.

THE DEATH OF CUPID: RECLAIMING THE WISDOM OF LOVE, DATING, ROMANCE AND MARRIAGE
by Nachum Braverman & Shimon Apisdorf
The Death of Cupid is divided into four sections: The Wisdom of Marriage, The Wisdom of Dating, The Wisdom of Sex and The Wisdom of Romance. This book speaks equally to singles in search of love and couples seeking to deepen their relationship.

"An insightful guide to discovering the beautifully deep potential of marriage."
John Gray Ph.D., Author, Men Are From Mars, Women Are From Venus

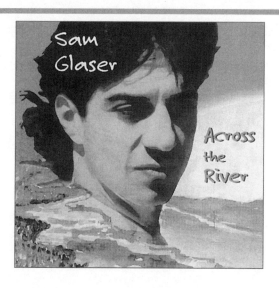

ABOUT THE AUTHOR

Shimon Apisdorf is an award-winning author whose books have been read by hundreds of thousands of people around the world. He has gained a world-wide reputation for his ability to extract the essence of classical Jewish wisdom and show how it can be relevant to issues facing the mind, heart and soul in today's world. Shimon grew up in Cleveland, Ohio, and studied at the University of Cincinnati, Telshe Yeshiva of Cleveland and the Aish HaTorah College of Jewish Studies in Jerusalem. He currently resides with his wife, Miriam, and their children in Baltimore. The Apisdorfs enjoy taking long walks, feeding the ducks, listening to the music of Sam Glaser and going to Orioles games. As for the Ravens: Forget it.

Shimon can be reached at ShimonA@idt.net